INTERNATIONAL LAW

The Rise of Russia as a Global Threat

Ben Wood Johnson

International Law
The Rise of Russia as a Global Threat

Ben Wood Johnson

TESKO PUBLISHING
Middletown, Pennsylvania

Published and printed in the United States of America by Tesko Publishing (Independent Press).
330 W. Main St, Unit 214, Middletown, PA 17057, United States of America

Paperback format

ISBN 978-1-948600-05-7 (paperback)
ISBN 1-948600-05-6 (paperback

Typeset in Garamond

Cover images (Canva.com)
Copyright holder not raced. Any copyright concerned should be directed to the address listed above. If contacted by the copyright holder, the publisher would make the necessary adjustments and provide proper credits in subsequent reprints. Cover illustration by Wood Oliver. For more information about the author, visit his website at www.drbenwoodjohnson.com

I dedicate this volume to my dear professor and mentor, **_Maitre Laventure._** He is the pillar of thirst to learn about the world. He introduced me to the world of politics. He paved the way for countless students of my generation to be curious about the world. He is part of a generation who experienced a promising world. He was optimistic for world peace and the rule of law. He inspired a similar passion in me.

CONTENTS

Contents

PREFACE

CORRUPTION IS A MAJOR problem in Russia. It has a link with everything in that society. It offers a bird's eye view about Russian affairs. Every year, *Transparency International* (a reputable organization) places Russia as one of the most corrupt states in the world.[1]

The rise of corruption is not the only issue facing the Russian State. The Russian government enjoys a delicate relation with most of its neighbors. Recently, the country's rapport with Ukraine worsened to a point of no return. The skirmish reached a crisis proportion. But Russia seemed undeterred to have its way in Ukraine.

In 2014, I sat a course about international law.[2] During that time, a lot was happening in the world. A lot was happening in Eastern Europe. Ukraine was in domestic disarray. The government became embroiled in a political

---

[1] Transparency International, "Transparency International - Russia," accessed September 21, 2018,
https://www.transparency.org/country/RUS.

[2] Mark Lawrence Schrad (at Villanova University) taught the course.

mayhem. Ukrainian officials could do little to tame the furor of the people.

The streets of Kiev experienced a wave of protests. The people demanded the immediate departure of their elected president at the time (Mr. Viktor Yannukovich). The government tried to resist the street pressure. It soon became obvious that the problem would only worsen.

I remember asking myself "What will happen to Ukraine." "What world powers could do to help the Ukrainian people," I wondered. But the slow response of the international community was shocking. Then, I realized that there is no rule of law within the international order. The crisis in Ukraine changed my perspective about the importance of international organizations designed to maintain peace. That experience inspired this work.

This compilation is not about Russia per se. the focus here is on International Law (IL). Indeed, there is a crisis within the international legal order. It seems like nobody cares about international rules. But what might explain that reality?

A likely answer is that international legal principles are ineffective. There is no real enforcement contrivance. It would not be an exaggeration to say that IL does not have real bearings in world affairs. Few nations consider IL a legal tool worthy of such title.

The text assesses the extent to which global institutions enjoy the power to punish belligerent nations. In this instance, I am referring to nations that regularly engage in conducts, which observers often consider problematic. The aim here is to examine conducts that may affect regional stability and global peace.

While this text is not thorough, it assesses issues that affect the international community. The idea is to explore whether international legal principles could deter or stop a nation from conducts that might lead to a broader conflict.

The book has four sections. The first introduces international law. The second provides an outline of the issues. The third elaborates on international law as a legal order. The forth examines the drawbacks of international institutions to enforce the law. The document includes a conclusion, a bibliography, an index, and author's notes.

The manuscript contains thirteen chapters. They are short, but to the point. The views are poignant, analytical, informative, intriguing, and captivating.

Although the text references scholarly works, it is not the result of a rigorous investigation. But it highlights striking issues in the literature. The major theme here is that international agencies are weak. As a result, they could not prevent global conflicts.

Regulating the behavior of powerful nations is a daunting task. As a result the extent (or even the relevance) of IL is, more often than not, negligible. Preventing nations that are economically and militarily powerful from chasing national interests at the expense of regional peace is almost impossible. International agencies, such as the United Nations (the UN and its Security Council), can be a huge disappointment.

Granted, the foregoing is a strong statement. Bear with me as I develop my argument, I will try to provide enough evidence to support the preceding claim.

Despite my concerns about IL, I do not think that it is useless. Even so, I reckon that there are many flaws in its enforcement means. The UN, for instance, is ineffective. In its current arrangement, this organization could not preserve global peace. We must reevaluate the reach of this entity.

As a force for good, the UN seldom prevents bad actors from imposing their will in the world. While few observers would question the legitimacy of this esteemed institution, countless others are skeptical about its deterrence power. Even the members of this prestigious entity often act in a way that undermines its relevance to preserve order within a fragile ecosystem.

The problem of enforcing international legal principles is more pervasive than a mere inability to deter powerful states from misbehaving on the world stage. Despite it all, the views I will outline throughout this compilation are important. They may shed some lights on the nature of the problem facing international institutions, such as the UN. I hope this book will entertain your intellectual curiosity.

—BEN WOOD JOHNSON
Pennsylvania, U.S.A.
November 2018

INTRODUCTION

RUSSIA'S AGGRESSIVE NATURE is undeniable. Would it be fair to single out Russia? I would say no. That is, no one country is a saint within the international order. Still, the presumption is that one country in particular is more belligerent within the international community. For some observers, that country is Russia.

Indeed, Russia often acts aggressively. At first glance, Russians do not care about IL. But Russia is not alone in its disdain for the international rule of law. We could consider the conducts of several powerful nations about IL. International institutions can also be unaffected by IL.

Countries like the United States, Israel, and the UN itself often act in ways that support the idea that IL is without importance within the international order. Over the last few years or so, they engaged in conducts that are harmful to peace. They provoked illegal wars, egregious human rights violations, illegal invasions, and economic starvation of other countries, just to name a few. But they do so under the guise of IL. Yet, when others (smaller countries) evoke international legal principles to condemn their actions, they seldom recognize the legitimacy of such laws. They often put in question the authority of IL. They often undermine the institutions that are supposed to act as the overseers of the world. Sadly, this is the nature of IL.

Powerful nations are likely to refute IL. However, they are likely to do so when it suits them the most. They may talk about the need for the rule of law. They may even boast their adhesion to such principles. Conversely, their actions often paint a different picture. Arguably, these countries only care about their own interests.

The reality of the international order is what it is. That is, the reach of IL is random. It is impulsive; it is weak.

The international legal order itself is not the result of a clear consensus. The unpredictable nature of this entity makes it precarious and feeble. There is not a clear understanding about international legal doctrines. As a result, international legal regimes are fragmented. That reality makes these institutions whimsical.

There is a lack of universality in IL. It is not surprising that forcing powerful nations (or belligerent leaders as the case may be) to obey international rules of law remains a daunting undertaken. Perhaps this reality could explain the reason international laws often have little or no real weight.

When it comes to waging wars or when it comes to the pursuit of interests (be they economic or else), there is no international rule of law. What is the importance of IL then? This is the fundamental question, which I am trying to answer in this book.

Granted, I could not respond to every question about IL. It is probable that I may not satisfy your curiosity. The polemic is more complex than most would admit.

Within the last few years or so, Russia took actions, which not only affected the stability of various countries in its region, but also highlighted the limits of global institutions to ensure order in certain parts of the world. The United States engaged in shameful conducts around the world. Other countries also misbehaved on the world stage. As hinted earlier, the UN itself often engaged in distasteful conducts. In my view, there is no high moral ground within the international order right now.

The previous reality makes IL an insignificant legal tool. But this is problematic. It poses a huge problem when it comes to preserving regional, if not global, peace. This calamity could not be direr in Eastern Europe. There, Russia rules over its neighbors in complete impunity.

Let us examine the nature of the Russian State in world politics. We must grasp the degree of the problem. We must assess, although not in depth here, the extent to which international institutions could help countries that find themselves in existential struggles. We must explore the degree to which such institutions could help appease the fear of nations that feel beleaguered. We must explore the degree to which international legal institutions enjoy any effect on powerful nations. We must evaluate how international principles mitigate world affairs.

It is also important to understand the fragility of international institutions. It is vital to understand the UN itself. This entity, in my view, is far from being autonomous or even independent. The UN exists because of the financial support of powerful countries. Excluding, similar nations also have a tendency to ignore international rules. Within that perspective, let us explore the extent to which IL could influence the behavior of powerful nations. Let us ponder on the following question:

a) Who should be the instigator of peace in the world?

b) Could there be lasting peace in the world when such reality could be so precarious?

c) What could they do about what many people make out as a growing threat Russia poses in Eastern Europe?

d) What could they do to improve the role of international institutions in reducing State behaviors either regionally or globally?

e) What is the true impact of legal rules or principles within the international order?

f) How we could contain the former Kievan State [3] (Russia) without triggering a Third World War?

g) What is the purpose of international institutions, such as the UN, in a predicament like the one Ukraine faces?

h) What is the purpose of an international legal order?

The issue of *international law* is complex. Many people consider IL an effective legal tool. But others do not think that way. I am part of the latter group.

Some observers are not sure that IL could help tame Russia. I share a similar viewpoint. Some political analysts do not see how world powers could deter Russia in, what they regard as, the country's search for world dominance. I will echo a similar sentiment throughout this document.

---

[3] See the book titled Russia and the Soviet Union: A Historical Introduction from the Kievan State to the present to learn more about how Russia constructed its identity in the world. John M. Thompson, *Russia and the Soviet Union: A Historical Introduction from the Kievan State to the Present* (Avalon Publishing, 2012).

Part 1

INTERNATIONAL LAW

CHAPTER 1

1. INTRODUCING INTERNATIONAL LAW

WHAT IS INTERNATIONAL Law? This is a straightforward question. However, the answer is not as simple as you might imagine it to be.

The term International Law (I describe it here as IL) stands for the law of the international order. That order reflects a slew of legal principles. They often come from domestic legal doctrines. Such principles, I must point out, guide international laws, rules, and norms. IL is, for lack of a better term, the law that governs international institutions. These laws oversee individuals, institutions, corporations, and nations.

For other observers, IL is a legal outline. It legitimizes or condemns certain behaviors within the international order. We could understand IL as sets of laws, which regulate the conduct of nations. The latter understanding is more relevant for our analysis here.

Applying international rule of law has its limits. Legal principles apply within a specific context. More often than not, such laws are applicable only when they suit the need of a particular country. We could say that IL is a whimsical legal tool. It often has little or no long-term effects on those who violate its most fundamental principles.

There is a need for IL. There is always a need to deter belligerent States from misbehaving on the world stage. The question is how could we achieve that goal without an effective international legal tool or instrument?

In Good Standing

Most people would argue that the international order is doing fine; it does not have any issues. It is in good standing, some might say. Nevertheless, others could argue to the contrary as well. I propose to do just that here.

Russia's recent actions in Ukraine support my position. I will also reference other world events to make the case that Russia is not the only culprit in violating IL. Other nations have little or no concerns for global legal principles. We must assess the present international legal model.

Before we delve further in the debate, let me point out that this work is not thorough. It only explores the reach of the rule of law. It examines the degree to which IL is inconsequential for world peace.

We must assess the role IL plays in the world. We must grasp the scope of the rule of law. Global legal instruments have all sorts of issues, many of which are a handicap for enforcing international laws.

The enforcement apparatus of IL is problematic. That reality stems from an array of issues. There can be no enforcement of a law if the perpetrator (or the violator) of the law itself is a powerful nation who holds a seat on the board of the entity whose job is to enforce the law. It is not surprising that there exists, what many consider, a double standard in the way international institutions enforce their own rules. Most often, those who are likely to violate the law are a source of revenue for those institutions. Thus, enforcing international rule of law could never be neutral.

The previous reality reinforces mistaken beliefs about IL. It affects the credibility of global institutions to enforce the law. That lack of partiality is also a huge flaw, which violators often use to undermine the same institutions that they themselves helped create. This is the nature of IL.

Powerful nations designed institutions specifically to uphold the law of the international without bias or without preferentiality. But these institutions are regularly under pressure to be partial when it suits the needs of certain countries. If these institutions were to assert their independence, the same nations who helped create them would also put in question their legitimacy. To sum up, this is the current nature of the international legal order.

Despite the enforcement issues mentioned earlier, punitive measures are embarrassingly ineffective. The international community relies on economic sanctions to punish belligerent nations. They often do so when a particular nation misbehaves either on the world stage or domestically. But retaliatory measures seldom deter belligerent governments, which have real power within the international order. This reality makes the influence of international institutions or agencies immaterial. The reason, I suppose, is that, many of these nations hold a stake in the United Nations (UN) itself.

Poorer [or smaller] nations seldom misbehave on the world stage. However, we could not say the same about richer or more powerful nations. It is only logical to assume that international institutions are incapable of preventing certain nations from violating agreed rules. They cannot do so in formal settings; they cannot do so in informal settings. What can they do, really? I am not sure.

Russia and International Law

Russia's recent intervention in Ukraine shows that IL can be depressingly useless. To reiterate, Russia is not the only country that violates international norms. Other nations routinely do the same. Some countries have undermined international principles to a point of jeopardizing the world order, which they want to maintain so dearly. For some reason, Russia is always in the news for what many consider draw-dropping conducts. For instance, the Russian annexation of Crimea is the most recent example, which might help explain the reason IL is out of order.

The United Nations (the UN) is a prestigious international body. It was perhaps created specifically, some might say, to tackle global problems. One of its missions, some might also echo, is to maintain world peace. The problem is that this task is almost impossible. The reason is that some of its most powerful members are always at the center of every skirmish in the world. These members often use the UN as a tool to achieve their goals.

In 2018, the United Nations Security Council had fifteen members. They included five permanent members.[4] Over the last few years, each of the five members engaged in conducts that the UN Security Council itself considers offenses toward international principles. Still, the punishment for such offenses had been less than desirable.

The United States, France, the United Kingdom, the Russian Federation, and China are among the most powerful members of the United Nations. These countries are the pillars of the international legal order (or IL). On the other hand, they are not exemplary actors within the global order.

Other countries often accused these international heavyweights of grave violations of international rules.[5]

---

[4] United Nations Security Council, "Members of the United Nations Security Council," accessed November 24, 2018, http://www.un.org/en/sc/members/.

[5] The following includes some of the articles or online resources concerning the types of violation committed by the five permanent members of the United Nations Security Council. Tim Daiss, "China Has Defied International Law, Now What? Experts Speak Out," Forbes, July 16, 2016, https://www.forbes.com/sites/timdaiss/2016/07/16/china-has-defied-international-law-now-what-experts-speak-out/. Merve Demirel, "International Law vs. Realpolitik in the South China Sea," *Huffington Post* (blog), March 21, 2017, https://www.huffingtonpost.com/entry/international-law-vs-realpolitik-in-the-south-china_us_58d08d1ee4b07112b647313c; Middle East Monitor, "Amnesty: France Violates International Law by Selling Arms to Egypt," *Middle East Monitor* (blog), October 17, 2018, https://www.middleeastmonitor.com/20181017-amnesty-france-violates-international-law-by-selling-arms-to-egypt/; Mark Curtis, "Britain's Violations of International Law," Mark Curtis, January 23, 2017, http://markcurtis.info/2017/01/23/britains-violations-of-international-law/; Ben Noble and Philippa Hetherington, "Russia

Yet, as permanent members within the UN Security Council itself, they get to decide the nature of other nations' conducts. It is like living in a topsy-turvy world. Yet, this is the reality of IL.

The most powerful members of the UN (in this case, the five permanent members) have a say on what international institutions do, when they do what they do, and for what purpose they do whatever it is that they do it. As a result, the UN often has little or no influence over the international order itself. The UN can be so powerless, notably when the violators of international rules or the perpetrators of certain conducts are among its most prestigious members. Again, this is the nature of IL.

Sanctioning a nation for misconduct is only effective when the concerned nation is economically dependent on others. These nations must also disapprove the conduct. Otherwise, the sanction, if it ever applied, would have little or no bearing on the concerned nation.

From here, the strategy is to punish violators via other means. A common approach is to impose economic sanctions on bellicose, but also economically powerless, nations. When a nation is a powerhouse, sanctions have little or no meaning. Sanctions have no real punitive values.

Doesn't Just Violate International Law – It Follows and Shapes It Too," The Conversation, accessed November 24, 2018, http://theconversation.com/russia-doesnt-just-violate-international-law-it-follows-and-shapes-it-too-92700; Curtis F.J. Doebbler, "Why the United States' Use of Force Against Syria Violates International Law," www.counterpunch.org, April 7, 2017, https://www.counterpunch.org/2017/04/07/why-the-united-states-use-of-force-against-syria-violates-international-law/.

Does IL have any relevance within the international order? The answer is no. There is enough evidence to support the notion that IL is weak. The rule of law is irrelevant within the current global order.

I will echo similar arguments throughout the text. If you would like to learn more, I encourage you to read further. There is more to the story of IL. Let us explore the issues further.

CHAPTER 2

2. IS RUSSIA A FRIEND OR A FOE?

COULD WE SAY THAT Russia is a friend? Is Russia a foe? Is Russia a belligerent nation? Depending on whom you ask these questions, you might get different responses. Answers might also contradict one another. Overall, there is no consensus in the literature.

Russia is a sensitive subject. Anti-Russian sentiments, mostly in Western regions, can be visceral. Thus, there is not a subjective means, which could help settle the debate.

Some might view the Russian State as an aggressor. In this case, Ukraine comes to mind. Others might see Russia as a friend. Here, China, Cuba, Venezuela, and several African nations come to mind. Somewhere in the middle, I would say, lies the truth.

Some might consider Vladimir Putin a savior. Here, Bashar al-Assad (from Syria) comes to mind. Anyway, I would not dispute similar views. To reiterate, somewhere in the middle lies the true nature of the Russian State or that of its leaders.

In the Western hemisphere (I must nevertheless point out), there is a unanimous sense of spurn toward the Russian State. Many fear Russian leaders in that part of the world. The perfect Russian belligerent, according to some observers, is Vladimir Putin himself.

The common understanding is that Putin is "Evil."[6] Whether this belief comes from any sound evidence is not the subject of this inquiry. It is incontestable that the Russian State often behaves recklessly. We could look at some of the conditions that might explain Russia's misbehavior in world politics.

The Russian State

While views about Russia are not always uniform across the globe, there is a reality. Few could refute it. Many Western Countries consider Russia an enemy or a potential rival. Fewer nations in Eastern Europe trust Russian leaders. Most heads of states in that region would not cooperate with the Russian State. They would not do business with Russia. When it comes to issues that may affect former Soviet States, the subject can be touchy.

Some countries would avoid facing Russia on any front, be it militarily or economically. Few regional politicians doubt the aggressive nature of the Russian State. Who could blame them? There is an irrefutable reality about Russia in Eastern Europe.

---

[6] Alexander Motyl, "Putin, Just Evil Enough," CNN, accessed July 8, 2017, http://www.cnn.com/2014/07/25/opinion/motyl-putin-is-evil/index.html.

Russia is a nuclear State. The country is a military giant. Until now, Russia seems locked down in the search for regional power, if not global dominance. By relying on that understanding alone, a country should never ignore or perhaps should never overlook concerns about the Russian State, principally if that country were to be a small Baltic State.

Russia has a tainted reputation in world politics. If one were to rely solely on recent reports citing the country's instrumentality domestically, regionally, or even internationally, we could make the case that Russia is on the verge. When it comes to regional peace and security, Russia is in the wrong direction. Russian officials, on the other hand, might point out unfair media coverage against their State.

Even though Russian leaders might have enough evidence to show a media bias against them, the country's records in Eastern Europe could be hard to refute. The State's recent incursion in Ukraine says a lot about Russia and its leaders. Some might say that Russia has little or no interest in global restraints. Russia's latest behaviors on the world stage suggest that Russian leaders have little or no concerns for international principles. To put it bluntly, Russia does not seem too concerned for the rule of law.

Growing Stronger

Russia is growing stronger each day. Both economically and militarily, the Russians are important players in the world these days. Perhaps Russian leaders feel invincible on the world stage. However, what might explain such a worldview, if it were to be true?

A likely answer is that international institutions, namely the UN, have little or no power to deter a nation like Russia. UN resolutions alone cannot stop a rogue actor or a rogue nation from misbehaving. Cert, the preceding statement could incite contentious viewpoints about the scope (or the bearing) of the rule of law. Nonetheless, this reality can also be self-evident.

Indeed, there is an atmosphere of *laissez-faire* in the international order right now. Some countries do whatever they please. Often, they do so under the watchful eye of international institutions, including the UN itself. At the same time, smaller nations often have no real recourse against powerful ones. This reality does not create an atmosphere of conviviality, which might be conducive to world peace and security.

The international community is a faction within the international order itself. As a global group, they could not tame States like Russia. What alternatives do they have? Russia is not an ordinary nation.

It is not clear whether one nation—on its own—could stop Russia. No country, even though it might be powerful, could single handedly deter the Russian State with a mere threat of economic sanction. Even with a military threat, that alone would not intimidate Russia. The state has a powerful military machine.

All hints suggest that international legal order does not work. Some might say that it is broken. International institutions cannot or could not dissuade a powerful State like Russia to obey IL. Thus, the Russian State could misbehave in complete impunity on the global stage. This is the nature of our current international legal instrument.

On the face of the mentioned reality, it is undeniable that international institutions are weak. Some analysts might also argue that the impotency of international agencies is by design. That is, they did not create the order so that it could be effective or efficient. Granted, this view is conspiratorial in nature. However, the powerlessness of international institutions to enforce their own laws could not be plainer. Perhaps there is some truth to the viewpoint that the international order is weak on purpose.

Recent events show that the Russian State holds little or no regards for international norms or rules of conduct. What could explain their attitude? In Eastern Europe, for instance, Russia rules over its neighbors with an unparalleled rigor. It often does so with complete impunity and under the eyes of the international community. The question worth asking is why that is the case. International organizations like the United Nations (UN) and the North Atlantic Treaty Organization (NATO) exist to enforce international legal principles.

Few observers have a clear understanding about the reason Russia appears unaffected by IL. What is also obvious is that when it comes to issues about former Soviet States, the Russian government is firm and, at times, bold in their approach. It is as if international rules do not apply to Russia in these regions.

Part 2

Containing Russia

CHAPTER 3

3. LACK OF MORAL SUPERIORITY

WHO COULD TAME the Russian State? Who has the authority to tell Russia that it cannot invade another country? Is there a nation that enjoys the political, the diplomatic, or perhaps the military ground to rebuke the Russians for their incursion in Crimea when such a conduct is not novel within the international order?

Who could punish Russia for misbehaving on the world stage? Who could claim a moral superiority in refuting Russia's conducts in Eastern Europe? At this point, answers are not clear. Are there other implications worth considering? I would say yes.

Indeed, a few ramifications are worthy of note in this case. The most striking complication has to do with the risk of a global conflict. I do not think that one nation alone could preserve peace in the world. In saying that, I reckon that one nation alone could disturb world peace.

When it comes to misconducts on the world stage, everyone's hands are dirty. Military aggression is the currency of the international order. No one country could claim ethical superiority when the foundation of many (if not all) superpower nations today comes from conducts similar to the ones the Russian State engaged in recent years.

It would not be an exaggeration to say that only the prospect of wars could deter a nation from engaging in aggressive conducts. There is always a need for conflicts. Accordingly, there could only be war as a way to ensure some form of peace (if we could call it that) in the present arrangement of the international order.

Every superpower nation within the international order today has a colonial past. For a better or worse, that past makes it almost impossible for similar nations to claim any moral higher ground. It makes it even more daring for any superpower nation to claim any right of hierarchy in world polity. They have to impose their worldviews on others. On the contrary, some nations are not always in line with the policies, the politics, or even the expectations of powerful States. In it lies the issue for IL.

The previously noted reality poses an interesting dilemma for international legalists. It poses a serious problem for IL itself. It undermines international legal principles. The question is how could the world be at peace when such a state is so fragile within the global order? I am not sure how to answer this question.

To be clear, I will not linger on the earlier questions. However, I will provide a few hints about my position. Of course, you might not share some of the views I will echo here. Anyway, I encourage you to keep this inquiry in mind as you navigate the text.

Hegemonic Pursuit

Being a Hegemon is not a flattering reputation. The term itself implies a supremacy over others. Hence, this is not a gratifying title under any circumstance.

We could have a debate about which country is the most evil in the world. We could agree to disagree about the most fearful dictator on the planet. What is undeniable is that Russia is among the most powerful nations in Europe today, if not the world over. That status alone makes of Russia a feared nation.

Russia's reputation is not just in Europe. The country is among the most dreaded nations in Asia. The same is true for the Middle East.

The fear that many feel for Russia, some might say, is reasonable, for it is not the result of a fantasy. There is enough evidence to support that sense of fright toward Russia. By referring to past conducts (even by looking at current behaviors), we could say that Russia can be unnecessarily aggressive. At a domestic level, many heads of state fear the Russian State. The Russians have no boundaries on what they could do throughout the region.

Even Russians themselves fear their government. For most observers, Russia is not a true democracy. Some view Russia as an authoritarian country. Within the current international order, some might say, Russia is alone. Countries that Western powers influence are unlikely to do business with Russia. The Russian State has fewer supporters (or allies) within the international community.

Russia is perhaps aware of its position in world politics. In the past, the Russian State used its military preeminence and its economic might to make a reputation for itself. In recent years, Russian leaders leveraged their influence in Eastern Europe in the same manner. They did so both economically and militarily. Perhaps their goal is to instill more fear in the region.

Russia is aware that others fear its military capacity. The same is true on the economic front. The view is that Russia is merciless toward its neighbors. From a military angle, some observers consider Russia as an omnipotent force. The country has one of the most powerful military apparatus in the world. To most observers, Russia poises itself as a formidable rival.

Over the years, Russian leaders earned many enemies in the Western world. The view in many Western political circles is that the Russian State has been acting as a bully. For the Russians, this view is arbitrary. Perhaps there is some truth there. Russia's record in Europe is telling about the rapport the country holds with its neighbors.

Russia and Eastern Europe have a long history. That record reflects a dependency guided mostly by fear and the threat of war. To this day, the chills of the cold war are still present in various parts of the region. That degree of harshness, as Marvin Kalb [7] put it, recently reached a freezing point.

When Putin entered Ukrainian territory in early 2014, most people, including Western political leaders, were both

---

[7] Marvin Kalb is a former journalist and Harvard professor who wrote a book about what he refers as an "Imperial Gamble" on the part of Vladimir Putin for seizing Crimea. Learn more about his book. See Marvin Kalb, *Imperial Gamble: Putin, Ukraine, and the New Cold War*, 2nd Print edition (Washington, D.C: Brookings Institution Press, 2015).

angry and disappointed.[8] For some reason, the default response was to go after Putin himself. Many world leaders criticized Putin. Some condemned the man for engineering, what they make out as, a return of East-West rhetoric.

World leaders fear the prospects of a Russian dominance in Europe. Many believe this reality would be damaging for the region. There is a sense that the Russian State should not have the leeway to achieve its goals in Eastern Europe in complete impunity.

After Russia entered Ukraine, the international community responded by threatening to impose "economic sanctions and diplomatic isolation," wrote Kalb.[9] According to Kalb, Russia's action in Crimea was a gamble; an *"Imperial Gamble,"* that is. It was a reckless gamble, even a dangerous one, Kalb further wrote.[10] But I think this view ignores or perhaps undermines the reality of the international order itself. Classifying Russia's action as a gamble misses the point about the country's true aims.

A Political Gamble

The Russians did not gamble when they entered Ukraine. Instead, it was a calculated move. They pushed the envelope to a breaking point. History has shown this is how Russia works.

When it comes to Eastern Europe, we could approach Russia's actions as a well thought out strategy to

---

[8] Ibid.

[9] Ibid., xi.

[10] Ibid.

undermine Western powers. Russia has a long-term goal in Eastern Europe. This is largely the case in the former Baltic States.[11]

In my view, the Russians know what they are doing in that part of the world. They provoke their own aggression in the region. Russia carefully calculated every move before making it. Perhaps this is a strategy for maximum results.

It is debatable whether every action the Russians undertake in Eastern Europe is not (or could not be) a gamble. There are noticeable effects to the way the Russians behave in the world. Their actions are not always on par with behaviors that might lead to world peace. Yet, the Russians, just like those who often violate international norms, seldom suffer the after-effects of their actions. To say it again, this is the nature of IL.

Perhaps Russia feels that its actions in Eastern Europe are legitimate. Perhaps the Russians see the region as their property. Russian officials may have a good rationale to hold such a view. A few precedents in history could corroborate their approach.

President James Monroe considered the Western Hemisphere, notably the Caribbean and Latin America, as America's backyard. Most people know this worldview as

---

[11] The term *Baltic States* usually refers to countries that are connected via the *Baltic Sea*. These countries include Latvia, Poland, Estonia, Russia, Denmark, Finland, Sweden, and Germany. To learn more, see James H. Bater and Romuald J. Misiunas, "Baltic States," Encyclopædia Britannica, inc., January 8, 2016, https://www.britannica.com/place/Baltic-states; Wikipedia, "Baltic Region," *Wikipedia*, June 3, 2018, https://en.wikipedia.org/w/index.php?title=Baltic_region&oldid=844232543.

"The Monroe Doctrine (1823)."[12] The Americans always evoke this argument to seize certain countries or to prevent others from doing so within the noted region. This was the case in Haiti, the Dominican Republic, and in parts of Latin America.

Perhaps Vladimir Putin also considers the Eastern part of Europe as Russia's backyard. We could call that view, the *"Putin Doctrine."* Whether implied or stated, Russia has conducted itself as if it considers Eastern Europe as its own field of influence.

Most countries in that part of the world, notably smaller nations, have a legitimate reason to fear Russia. They have a reason to dread the country's military and economic rise. Many of these small States were once part of the Russian empire. It is only logical that Russia would feel a sense of ownership over many of these nations. At this cross road in history, Russia seems resolved to revive its former empire as it was during its heyday.

Another angle is also worth pointing out in the debate. In that case, Russia has a political *sine qua non*. Russian leaders appear determined to protect their borders at all costs. Some might say that the Russian State sees itself in

---

[12] The Monroe doctrine (1823) reflects the notion that European powers should refrain themselves from intervening in the Western Hemisphere. This part of the continent belongs to America. Learn more about the Monroe Doctrine by visiting the following links. Our Documents, "Our Documents - Monroe Doctrine (1823)," accessed November 22, 2018,
https://www.ourdocuments.gov/doc.php?flash=true&doc=23; The Editors of Encyclopaedia Britannica, "Monroe Doctrine: History, Elements, & Facts," Encyclopedia Britannica, October 26, 2018, https://www.britannica.com/event/Monroe-Doctrine.

an existential battle against powerful nations, including the US, France, Australia, Germany, and Great Britain, to name a few. There might be some truth to that understanding as well.

There is a genuine reluctance in the international community to allow Russia to become a superpower. There is an irrefutable resistance to allow Russia to play a larger role on the world stage, at least just as the former Union of Soviet Socialist Republics (U.S.S.R.) once did it. [13] Therefore, the race is on to stop the Russians from reclaiming a long lost reign over the world.[14]

Taming the Russian State

Russian leaders are, at first glance, on a mission to revive the country's influence in world polity by whatever means necessary. This is the essentiality of the debate. The only tool available to carry out that task is IL. However, this legal machinery is, at least now, dysfunctional.

Vladimir Putin, some believe, is set in his pursuits. Seemingly, he wants to put Russia back on the map as a superpower. As a direct result of Russia's recent conducts in Ukraine, the only way to deter its rise is via military

---

[13] The USSR was a combination of a numbers of countries, including Russia itself, Ukraine, Kazakhstan, Moldova, the Baltic States, and the Central Asian Republics.

[14] To learn more, please see Team Novelguide, "Rise of Superpowers After WWII," Novelguide, accessed July 8, 2017, http://www.novelguide.com/reportessay/history/general-history/rise-superpowers-after-wwii.; Larisa Epatko, "Once a Superpower, How Strong Is Russia Now?," PBS NewsHour, January 13, 2017, http://www.pbs.org/newshour/updates/how-strong-is-russia-now/.

means. Some could also argue that this approach would be a fruitless undertaken. Such a demarche would be bad for world peace in the end.

No doubt, Russia is rising. But its ascension represents a global threat. Yet, we could not treat Russia as an average belligerent nation. There is more at stake in the country's behaviors. There is the potential for a greater conflict in demarches to contain Russia. The Russian State was once a Titan among Titans.

Russia has a legacy of military conflicts. That past affords its leaders a glare of ruthlessness. That is why many observers view Russia as a foe or a potential of that. Still, the idea that we could defeat the country easily on a battleground is unrealistic. This reality brings up an interesting question. That is, what is the degree to which other nations could tame Russia?

Controlling Russia is in the agenda of most Western powers. However, the degree to which this aim is achievable remains uncertain. Even so, the core issue worth examining is the extent to which international norms, global agencies, or institutions could prevent a country like Russia from acting belligerently on the world stage. At this point, it is unlikely that other nations could tame Russia.

Despite the previous understanding, this work does not offer an empirical assessment of the reality of the international order. Here, I will avoid unnecessary speculations. But for the sake of clarity, let us examine, though not meticulously, the role that international bodies like the UN may play in world polity.

We could assess the role similar institutions play in deterring *Rogue States* from misbehaving. Let us assess the effectiveness of their behaviors. We could examine the degree to which the UN Security Council could have stopped Russia from annexing Crimea. Of course, we have to reckon that Russia and Ukraine have a long history. Here, however, there is no need to examine the historical bond between the two countries.

Let us revisit the issues that led to what we could call a *"Russian power grab"* in Ukraine. We could also call it a *"Russian land grab."* In this context, my argument is that we must grasp the reason many across Eastern Europe despise Russia. [15] Let us examine the implications of Russia's potential regional dominance. Let us explore the position Russia espoused in world affairs since Vladimir Putin came to power.[16] Let us examine the reason Russia developed an irrefutable discount for international rule of law.

---

[15] Deterrent weaponry may include a nuclear arsenal or other forms of lethal delivery systems, such as a battery of missile or other capabilities.

[16] See the "Putin and the Rise of Russia" to learn how Russia regained its superpower status in the world after the collapse of the Soviet Union Michael Stuermer, *Putin and the Rise of Russia* (Pegasus Books, 2010).; Marcel H. Van Herpen, *Putin's Wars: The Rise of Russia's New Imperialism* (Rowman & Littlefield, 2015); Charles Clover, *Black Wind, White Snow: The Rise of Russia's New Nationalism* (Yale University Press, 2016); Marshall Goldman, *Oilopoly: Putin, Power and the Rise of the New Russia* (Oneworld Publications, 2010); Steven Lee Myers, *The New Tsar: The Rise and Reign of Vladimir Putin* (Simon and Schuster, 2015).

CHAPTER 4

4. RUSSIA AND THE LAW

DOES THE RULE OF LAW apply to Russia? For some, the answer is a resounding yes. For others, however, the answer may vary, depending on whom you ask.

What might explain that discouraging reality? We could consider a few explanations. For instance, what makes up the rule of law within the international order is not clear.

Other issues are worth considering here as well. For example, how international rules and principles should apply is unclear. When the law should apply is often the subject of intense debate. The extent or the scope of the law itself is equally uncertain. In other words, there is no consensus about the characteristics of the rule of law within the international system. There is always disagreement about the possible motives of those seeking to enforce the law.

The notion of a global order is controversial. There is not a clear understanding about what such an order should be. There is no definite consensus about what the rule could be within the [current] format of what most regularly refer as the *International Community*.[17]

Within the international milieu itself, most nations do as they please. Some could become unnecessarily annoyed when it comes to finding the means to protect their own interests. That is the reason it is important to explore the role of international institutions in creating the conditions for Russia to misbehave on the world stage.

To echo a previous event, Russia annexed a popular region in Ukraine (Crimea) in 2014. That act sent shivers down the spines of many world leaders. At the time, there was a sense that Russia would go in an annexation spree in Eastern Europe.

Voices resounded throughout the region to demand international institutions, namely the UN, to stop the Russian madness. At the time, however, the UN could do little or nothing in this international mêlée. Equally, there were little or no disagreements in most Western countries about the nature of the political (or the social) upheaval, that embroiled the Ukrainian State.

The common understanding is that Russia's action in Crimea was an egregious military aggression. Most political analysts contended that it was a deliberate violation of the sovereignty of another nation. Yet, international institutions, such as the UN, could do little to nothing to stop Russia.

From the Russian viewpoint, Russia did what it had to do to protect its people. That is, the Russians had an

---

[17] Here, I will use the terms "International Community" and "International system" interchangeably.

obligation to intervene in Ukraine. Protecting the Russian-speaking population, the Russian State claimed at the time, was supreme in the region after the fall of *President Viktor Yannukovich*. Protecting individuals whom have a link with Russia is what Russian officials (including Vladimir Putin himself) evoked as the core reason for annexing the Crimean Peninsula.[18]

Analytical Limits

As a side note, let me point out that the present edition does not debate the extent to which Russian leaders had valid concerns in Crimea. There is no need to explore the degree to which an invasion (or even the annexation) of part of an independent State was the answer to Russia's need for safety or security. I will not take this approach here. Nonetheless, we must explore the role international institutions could play in preventing conflicts from intensifying in Ukraine.

In addition, we must revisit the manner in which the upheaval in Eastern Europe captivated the world. We must discover what they did (or what they could do), at least internationally, to stop the Russian military from marching onto Ukrainian territory. We must examine the degree to which these events mobilized the international community in a unified chorus against the Russian State. We must explore the actions international institutions posed, which aims were to provide a sense of tranquility in the region.

---

[18] Many observers consider Russia's reason to invade Crimea as an unjustified pretext.

To reiterate, this book does not examine the chaotic liaison Russia enjoys with international institutions. It does not explore the nature of the likeness that exists between the Russian State and countries like the United States, France, and Great Britain. It does not examine the conditions, which appeared conducive for Russia's aggressive conducts in Ukraine, if not in Eastern Europe. It does not explore the political disagreement among the Russians, the Americans, and the United Nations.

While the analysis presented here is not exhaustive, it does not lack intellectual merits. This work is relevant enough to contribute in the literature. Anyway, I invite you to consider the previously stated limits, as you navigate the remaining portions of this text.

Why Examining Russia

Russia has always been on the news. Others often accuse the State of mischievous behaviors. They often blame the country for all sorts of international escapades, including hacking the recent U.S. Elections.[19] To say it again, I will not examine the degree to which the claims regularly levied against the Russian State reflect sound criticisms. I will not explore whether these views are the results of facts.

---

[19] See *Assessing Russian Behaviors and Intentions in Recent US Elections.*, Intelligence Community Assessment (Office of the Director of National Intelligence, National Intelligence Council, 2017); Daniel Schearf, "Russia Dismisses US Hacking Allegations as 'Election Campaign Instrument,'" *Voice of America News/FIND*, October 8, 2016; Eliza Collins, "Yes, 17 Intelligence Agencies Really Did Say Russia Was behind Hacking," *USA Today (Online)*, October 21, 2016; V. O. A. News, "US Accuses Russia of Hacking Attempts on Political Groups," *Voice of America News/FIND*, October 7, 2016.

Few people could defend Russia without undermining certain realities about the State itself. One could not ignore the country's conducts within the last two decades or so. Some observers have offered arguments, which, depending on personal perspectives, clear Russia's conducts on the world stage. There is the view that Vladimir Putin is not such a bad person after all.[20]

Most Western politicians both love and despise Russia. The same is true when it comes to those seeking to preserve their financial interest in Russia. That love-hate marriage, some might argue, is the results of economic priorities. It could be the results of political ideologies. The line between the two is blurry.

Some observers have argued that there is unnecessary hysteria about Russia, prominently in the United States. While I will not address the nature of such a claim, I must point out that most analysts believe that the present state of panic toward Russia is baseless. The fear against the Russian State is the result of a made out political development, some say.

Other analysts claim that misunderstandings about Russia are in error. That is, Russia is not a foe. Some have even contended that such a view of the Russian State is superfluous.

---

[20] Adam Taylor, "Analysis | The Americans Who Think Vladimir Putin Isn't so Bad," *Washington Post*, July 28, 2016, sec. World Views Analysis Interpretation of the news based on evidence, including data, as well as anticipating how events might unfold based on past events, https://www.washingtonpost.com/news/worldviews/wp/2016/07/28/the-americans-who-think-vladimir-putin-isnt-so-bad/.

Blaming or defending Russia is not necessarily an independent act. An ideology is always at the source of the positions many people have adopted either pro or against the Russian State or its leaders. In the United States, for instance, Democrats criticize Russia, while Republicans adopt a more favorable stance toward the country.

Defending Russia

In academia, many scholars sought to defend Russia. [21] Perhaps some did not take it on their own to do so. In this case, academicians and professionals in world affairs often point out that misjudgments vis-à-vis Russia generally come from mischaracterizations about the nature or the air of Vladimir Putin himself, Russia's current Head of State.

Mark Lawrence Schrad, an expert in Russian politics, argues that, "Vladimir Putin is not a Super villain."[22] While this view is not in the majority, it is probably not in error. It is not the result of fanciful understandings about the relations, which the Russians enjoy with the Americans. This view, perhaps its reverse as well, is among the many points of disputes that people often levy against Russia.[23]

---

[21] Some have expertise in world politics.

[22] Mark Lawrence Schrad, "Vladimir Putin Isn't a Supervillain," *Foreign Policy* (blog), March 2, 2017, https://foreignpolicy.com/2017/03/02/vladimir-putin-isnt-a-supervillain/.

[23] Please keep in mind that I do not debate that view in depth in the present work.

The common beliefs include the view that the Russians are bad people; they are villains; we should not trust them.[24]

On the other hand, some analysts have sought to draw a line between the Russian State itself and Russian leaders. When they criticize Russia, they suggest, they do not seek to rebuke the Russian people. Rather, they seek to call out the direction Russian leaders have espoused in world politics or even domestically.

The argument is that even though Russia has problems, the country is not different from other nations. Instead, they say, Russian leaders are the problem. They do not seem willing to fix the issues that plague Russian society.

Other observers refute the notion that President Vladimir Putin is not a *"Super villain."* Most pundits in the Western world regularly caricature Mr. Putin as a dangerous Villain. Some say that Russian officials would enjoy a reputation as *"Villains."* Of course, it is not clear that Mr. Putin would enjoy the title of a *"Super villain."* That understanding, I would argue, is worthy of our attention.

As they say, "actions speak louder than words." This popular adage could explain how Russia often conducts itself on the world stage. If we were to judge Russia by evoking its behaviors in Eastern Europe, any description of the State would be somber. Most Russian officials would fall in the category of belligerent leaders, if not *"Super Villains."* Pointing that out, I must say, does not form an unprovoked poke against the Russians on my part.

---

[24] Certainly, these views are the results of stereotypes about the Russian people in general. However, Westerners mostly hold these views.

Over the years, Russia has displayed an unfathomable slight for the rule of law. The country is uncontrollable regionally. By that understanding, Russia is irrefutably untamable, at least globally. This reality also signals a larger issue within the international order. By any assessment, IL is not an effective legal tool. Thus, IL is incapable of deterring a nation like Russia from misbehaving either regionally or globally.

We must explore the homogeneity Russia enjoys with its neighbors. We must review the nature of the praise the country entertains with many of its allies and its enemies. Let us make sense of that contingency.

CHAPTER 5

5. THE RISE OF A GLOBAL THREAT

AFTER THE FALL OF the Soviets (in the early 1990s), many people were quick to dismiss a possible resurgence of the U.S.S.R. in any way, shape, or form. A crisis resulted after the Soviet Union fell apart in 1991.[25] Most observers saw this epoch as a tumultuous moment in the country's political history.[26] Back then, few people saw the newly created Russian Federation as a threat to world peace.

By the late 1990s, most observers considered Russia a failed State. There was some sympathy for the nation as a whole. The future was bleak for the State.

---

[25] Joshua S. Goldstein, *International Relations*, 6 edition (New York: Longman, 2004), 92.

[26] Rajan Menon, "How the Tumultuous '90s Paved the Way for Putin's Russia," *The New York Times*, April 10, 2017, sec. Book Review, https://www.nytimes.com/2017/04/10/books/review/who-lost-russia-cold-war-peter-conradi.html.

There were skepticisms about the degree to which Russian leaders would be able to adhere to democratic principles. Russia's institutions were in turmoil. Few people predicted that the State would enjoy any form of political stability. The country experienced all sorts of issues. Corruption was considered the biggest problem facing the state. Russian officials had a fondness for corruption.

During its creation, the Russian State (or the Russian Federation) was struggling to prevent the union from dilapidating. For several years that followed the Soviet dissolution, States after States sought to detach themselves from Soviet dominion. From both a military angle and economically, the country was a mess.

Out of the ashes of the Soviet Union rose Vladimir Putin. It was almost prophetic. Observers saw the collapse of the U.S.S.R. as a pedestal on which Putin consolidated his political power network.[27] In the early 2000s, there was a political vacuum in the country, which few politicians could fill.

To the dismay of most Western observers, Vladimir Putin became the darling of Russia. Putin became a rising political star, whom few could undermine. Little by little, Putin built a new phase in Russian politics.

Most analysts agree that the political reality in Russia toward the end of the 1990s led to "Putinism." To this day, the Putin brand is a political *savoir-faire* that few have

---

[27] Ibid.

matched in Russian politics. An even fewer number of politicians have been able to challenge that approach.[28]

Vladimir Putin is often herald as the new *Czar* in Russia's history. Many consider him a strong leader domestically. Putin's power and influence are, on the face of it, without boundaries. The geographic borders of the Russian State are not enough to contain Putin's reach. Since Putin, Russia's influence in the world has grown.

A Global Powerhouse

There is a new Russia in town. Fast forward to 2018; there is a new reality within the international order. Russia is a new global force.

The new-fangled Russian-swagger was obvious during the Ukraine debacle. It is also irrefutable in Syria. Russia "put up a united front" behind Bashar al-Assad, a leader many in the Western world regard as a "troubled tyrant" or a "ruthless despot."[29] But it is not clear the reason Russia supports the Syrian regime. Many have speculated about possible motives, including arms sales, strategic military access in the Mediterranean port of Tartus, and Vladimir Putin's own fear of State collapse.[30]

---

[28] I use the term "Putinism" to connote the political dominance of Vladimir Putin in Russia politics, both domestically and internationally.

[29] Jon Lockett, "Why Does Russia Support Syria and Bashar Al-Assad and Who Else Is Involved in the Syrian Civil War?," The Sun, October 9, 2018, https://www.thesun.co.uk/news/6006649/russia-support-syria-air-strikes-response/.

[30] Fiona Hill, "The Real Reason Putin Supports Assad," *Brookings* (blog), March 25, 2013, https://www.brookings.edu/opinions/the-real-reason-putin-supports-assad/.

There is more to the issues in Syria than most would admit. In any event, Russia has proved that it is a powerhouse in every sense of the word. Since the country's rebirth in early 2000s, Russia has reasserted itself on the global stage. The country did so despite its tumultuous political history. For a good or bad, the Russian State rebuilt itself in ways that few Western analysts foresaw.

Nowadays, there is a much more depressing tune when observers speak about Russia. Many people believe that the Russian State could play a role in hampering peace in Europe. Some people believe that Russia could become an uncontrollable global threat. The reason, many observers say, Russia is "out of control."[31] There could be a little bit of truth in that view.

What could explain the reason the Russian State seems prone to engage in mischievous conducts in Eastern Europe? I could not offer a definite answer here. I could only speculate. Observers could refute any answer provided in this text to the nth degree.

Russia's actions, at least globally, could lead to a major international conflict. Critics have pointed out that the Russian State had been acting in ways that contrived efforts for regional peace. Again, there is some truth in that understanding. Let us examine the origins of that fear.

---

[31] This understanding is echoed by Paul A. Goble, a longtime specialist on ethnic and religious questions in Eurasia. See his piece at: Paul A. Goble, "'Situation in Russia Is Rapidly Getting out of Control,' Five Leading Moscow Experts Say," *Euromaidan Press* (blog), September 16, 2017, http://euromaidanpress.com/2017/09/16/situation-in-russia-is-rapidly-getting-out-of-control-five-leading-moscow-experts-say-euromaidan-press/.

To what extent, if any, Russia forms a threat to international peace and security. Most of the country's escapades often occur regionally. What is it that we could do, to say the least internationally, to tame Russia's aggressive stance across Eastern Europe?

No doubt, Russia is a belligerent nation. Is that enough reason to quarantine the Russian State itself? I am not sure.

It is important to point out that few nations could tame Russia. We could make the argument that not even powerful international institutions, such as the United Nations, could exert a control over the country's regional grip. Taming Russia (or the hope to do that) could only lead to war.

Russian Belligerence

By most assessments, Russia is seeking both regional and world dominance. For many years, the State engaged in conducts, which some would describe, rightfully so I might add, as aggressive. Such behaviors, some could also argue, have had negative impacts on IL in ways unimaginable.

The Russian's military *sortie* in Ukraine set the wrong precedent for world peace. This act was a violation of the sovereignty of another nation without even a provocation. It is worth admitting that Russia is not the only problem in the world right now. North Korea, some observers might say, is up to something sinister.

The North Korean regime recently tested several Inter Continental Ballistic Missiles (also known as ICBM), which the United States government via its Secretary of State at the time (Rex Tillerson) strongly condemned.[32] Officials in Pyongyang (the country's largest city and capital) claimed that the test was successful. No doubt, Western leaders are wary about North Korea. Some observers are skeptical about what will happen next.[33]

The stakes are high. Even Alaska could be on the line.[34] Recent reports suggest that the North Korean regime has the means to target a good portion of the United States.[35]

Despite the threat posed by North Korea, most Westerners have more concerns for Russia. The understanding is that the threat the Russian State poses is more menacing than any form of danger other States could make up. The reason, some have argued, is that Russia is already a nuclear power. In addition, the country has a powerful military apparatus. These realities alone makes

---

[32] Barbara Starr, Ryan Browne, and CNN, "As US, SK Drill, Tillerson Seeks Action on NK," CNN, July 4, 2017, http://www.cnn.com/2017/07/04/politics/us-officials-meet-north-korea-missile-launch/index.html.

[33] Elise Hu, "After North Korea's ICBM Launch, Now What?," NPR.org, July 5, 2017, http://www.npr.org/sections/parallels/2017/07/05/535465234/after-north-koreas-icbm-launch-now-what.

[34] Ibid.

[35] Deutsche Welle (www.dw.com), "Which US Cities Could North Korea's Ballistic Missile Hit?," DW.COM, July 29, 2017, https://www.dw.com/en/which-us-cities-could-north-koreas-ballistic-missile-hit/a-39881831; Tom O'Connor, "North Korea Says Nuclear Weapons Only Target U.S., Not Russia, China or South Korea as Talks Begin," January 19, 2018, https://www.newsweek.com/north-korea-nuclear-weapons-only-target-us-not-russia-china-south-talks-775589.

Russia a potential foe, if not, Russia could become a formidable military opponent.

Russia's incursion in Ukraine was probably a deliberate act. It was perhaps a part of a well-orchestrated effort to undermine the NATO Alliance. Others pointed out it was perhaps a calculated effort to undermine the international community. In practical terms, Russia's military behaviors in Eastern Europe are more alarming than most would admit. At first sight, the rise of Russia is part of a more pressing issue, if not an existential threat, facing many nations in that part of the world (that is, Eastern Europe). For most, Russia is a growing menace for regional peace, if not the world over.

In all fairness, I must echo that Russia is not the only nation that causes tensions within the global order. As noted earlier, North Korea is a problem, which few could deny. The United States in particular undertook many efforts to tame Pyongyang as ferociously as possible.

Apart from North Korea, most observers consider States like Iran and Syria as potential impediments to world peace. It is no secret that these countries have a geopolitical stake, which often dictates their behavior in their respective regions. It is not surprising that people often caricature the leaders of these countries as villains. Some observers label their States as safe havens for terrorist groups (or potential villains) or a threat for peace and security of other states. They often classify these countries as *Rogue Nations.*[36]

---

[36] The term *"Rogue States"* could be defined in the following manner. According to worldatlas.com, the term "refers to a country that is keen

The US vowed to sanction individuals (or companies) who engage in expansion behaviors with countries like Iran. A potential rise of Iran on the world stage evokes real fears in Washington. There is a deliberate effort to keep latent *Rogue Nations*, so-called, under a magnifying glass.

Unquestionably, the term "rogue" is an arbitrary way of grouping nations that do not fall in line with Western expectations. It is also an effort of classifying countries that act outside international norms or the rule of law altogether. For some, however, it is a badge of honor.

Many people consider several nations as impending threats to world peace. These countries include, but not limited to, Iran, North Korea, and Syria. They view Iran in particular as a prospective problem for American Interests in the Middle East. Both Israel and the United States hope to derail the Iranian's ambition to gain a nuclear arsenal. The Americans also hope to prevent the Iranian government from having any influence in the region.[37]

---

to deliberately and purposefully commit transgressions and break international laws and policies that are meant to ensure peace globally." Brian Kasyoka Musili, "What Is a Rogue State? (WorldAtlas)," WorldAtlas, August 1, 2017, https://www.worldatlas.com/articles/what-is-a-rogue-state.html.

[37] The website known as "Iran Business Risk" lists a series of violations Iran committed over the years. The website argues that Iran should never be trusted. Iranian violation of international laws treaties and conventions on various issues, including disarmament, diplomatic and consular relations, terrorism, human rights, civil and political rights, rights of the child, and UN organization violations, just to name a few. See the website in the following link. Iran Business Risk, "The Islamic Republic of Iran's Violation of Treaties and Multilateral Agreements," UANI, accessed November 27, 2018, /violation-of-treaties.

The American government adopted several legislations, which came about as a way to derail Iran on various fronts, including politically, militarily, and economically. American officials sent a clear message to other countries. The understanding is that no responsible countries should engage in business with belligerent nations, notably the Iranian State. In a 2005 act, which name is the Iran, North Korea, and Syria Nonproliferation Act Sanctions, [38] the Americans made it clear that they would impose severe penalties on individuals or institutions for the transfer to or buy from Iran, North Korea, and Syria. [39]

Despite the made out threats from other nations, the common belief is that Russia is among the most urgent issues facing the world. The belief is that Russia allied itself with the noted countries. Many in the Western world are certain that Russia has the potential to project an even more menacing threat in the Western Hemisphere.

This strange state of affair between Russia and other world powers is alarming. Some observers have argued that we must control Russia before it is too late. The pervading belief is that it is important to tame the Russian State at all costs. The problem is that containment initiatives may come with great risks.

One of such dangers is the possibility for a global conflict or even a *Third World War*. I am not sure that most Western nations would like to bear the responsibility of a

---

[38] It is also known as the INKSNA

[39] Diplomacy In Action U.S. Department of State, "Iran, North Korea, and Syria Nonproliferation Act Sanctions (INKSNA)," accessed July 8, 2017, https://www.state.gov/t/isn/inksna/.

large-scale war similar to a *World War*. In this regard, it would not be odd to say that most world powers do not want to provoke an irreversible global military quarrel.

The question is what could they do to tame Russia? Is Russia on the wrong side of history? Should we fear the Russian State? I would say no to these questions. I could not support demarches that might lead to hostilities among nations. The possibility for an intercontinental clash among superpower nations is too high.

The Risk of a Global Conflict

The international order is facing an important dilemma. On the one hand, some of the most powerful States within the order, including the United States and Great Britain, would like to tame Russia. On the other hand, there are few alternatives to carry out that goal without inducing a major world conflict.

As already mentioned throughout this text, Russia is a powerful State both politically and militarily. It could go toe-to-toe with any world power. Therefore, undermining Russia globally may prove difficult, if not strategically risky both politically and militarily. What could they do realistically? I am not sure.

The world could not sit idly by and let the Russian State acts as it pleases, in specie when it comes to the safety of Eastern Europe. Many nations are not sure about Russia's true intents in the region. There is a sense of urgency in some circles. Of course, there is the prospective for a wide scale conflict if we were to do nothing to cut off Russia's growing power and influence.

Within the last few years, the world experienced an array of minor, but important, conflicts. These series of military skirmishes suggest that a larger conflict might be on the making. The question worth asking here is to what extent the world should live in anxiety because of Russia. What is the threat Russia poses to peace, considering the existence of other threats.

Most political analysts would argue that Russia represents a dangerous precedent for peace within the global order. I would not refute that view. It would not be fair to blame the Russians alone for the ills of IL. In my view, IL is now a means for chaos. Of course, it was supposed to create the atmosphere for peace. It is undeniable that IL is ineffective. Even so, the issues are much more fundamental than they appear.

We must grasp the degree to which international institutions (for example, the UN) have enough influence to prevent conflicts among nations, be they powerful or not. When conflicts occur, what could they do to exert a control over the parties involved? Right now, international institutions are incapable of instilling order in a chaotic world.

It is not clear how IL could contain the Russian State. I could not say that Russia is on the wrong side of history. Perhaps it is a matter of perspective. On the other hand, the prognostics are bleak.

Ostensibly, Russia has a long-term goal. I do not know what it is. Considering the country's recent behaviors, one could presume that Russia wants total control over certain smaller States. Perhaps the Russians want to dominate

Eastern Europe. Perhaps Russia wants complete regional dominance in that part of the world.

My point here is that Russia is not an angel within the international order. Again, it would not be fair to label the Russian State as the only source of problems in the world. So long as domestic interests guide powerful nations, peace would always be a futile pursuit anywhere in the world.

There is little or no indication that international institutions, such as the UN, could make a difference when it comes to deterring nations such as North Korea, Iran, and Russia, just to name a few of course, from misbehaving. Presently, the UN has little or no influence on powerful nations to prevent them from creating a climate of instability in places where they feel that their interest is at stake. By that logic, IL is almost like a decorative legal instrument.

The Need for International Order

As I sought to show in the previous outline, international legal principles are irrelevant in world affairs. Most global institutions enjoy a limited influence in world polity. They lack the power (or the influence) to impose the rule of law. Thus, international rules have limited effects on the so-called *"Rogue Nations."*

There could not be lasting peace in the world unless IL becomes a more consequential tool to deter bad behaviors. IL must be omnipotent within the international order. Therefore, there is always a need for IL.

It is important to instill confidence in smaller nations about the need of international institutions. It is necessary to make IL a neutral legal instrument. It is equally important to reassure beleaguered States that IL would help them when they need it the most. Strengthening IL is indispensable to control powerful institutions—be they State or non-State actors—from misbehaving in the name of peace and security.

Presently, most international institutions lack the enforcement power to make a real difference in world politics. Some observers have criticized the United Nations for its double standard in the way it enforces international rules. It is likely to do so when it comes to complaints related to human rights and other abuses.[40] Some observers believe that the way they enforce IL as an embarrassment.[41] Many have called for an independent oversight over the UN Security Council; most people expressed concerns for the institution's five permanent members.[42]

It would not be fanciful to say that IL or most international institutions enjoy little or no relevance in world affairs. It is not surprising that smaller nations hope to buy as much influence as possible within the international system. Others appear determined to get a

---

[40] Denis J. Halliday, "The United Nations: The Embarrassment of International Law," *Medicine, Conflict, and Survival* 18, no. 4 (December 2002): 346–54, https://doi.org/10.1080/13623690208409644; IHH Humanitarian Relief, "Falk: Double standards in international law," IHH Humanitarian Relief Foundation, February 11, 2012, https://www.ihh.org.tr/en/news/falk-double-standards-in-international-law-1472; John Carey, "The United Nations' Double Standard on Human Rights Complaints," *American Journal of International Law* 60, no. 4 (October 1966): 792–803, https://doi.org/10.1017/S0002930000105883.

[41] Halliday, "The United Nations."

[42] Ibid.

footing at the UN itself. For instance, a non-permanent Council member could levy significant influence on this institution.

Belligerent nations are fixed. Many hope to become invincible within the international system. The plan perhaps is to become powerful enough to enforce the laws that benefit them. This approach would not necessarily be appealing to the global community as a whole.

Most countries want a fierce reputation. Some want other to fear them. The question is whether we should lump Russia in that category. I would say yes. I admit that the preceding is an open-ended question.

A grave danger hangs over the world. Powerful countries seem determined to increase their nuclear arsenal. Getting destructive weaponry (including, but not limited to, nuclear weapons and biological stockpiles) become a common pursuit within the international order. The problem is that the UN often has little or no means to deter such efforts. This reality invites us to question the reason many are certain that we need IL.

Some might say that it is mainly to uphold peace in the world. Would they be right? Is there a secret agenda to IL? I am not sure how to answer.

This reality invites another question. That is, why IL seems so weak? Should we blame powerful nations for the impotence of IL? I would say yes. Their actions seem conducive to making international legal rules irrelevant. Their refusal to uphold international principles weakens international institutions at any level.

Some of these nations also seem determined to undermine the UN. They are likely to do so when it suits them the most. War, I would argue, is a business, which—unfortunately, I might add—the UN with its current influence could not prevent, control, or even stop. It would be naïve to think that IL alone could prevent the world from descending into complete anarchy. Even so, we must effort to change that reality.

International institutions enjoy an even lesser influence on powerful States, including, but not limited to, the United States, Great Britain, France, and Israel, to name a few. The same is true for the Russian State. With all that said, several key issues remain unascertained in the debate. Let us revisit a few of them in the next few chapters.

CHAPTER 6

6. AN ALARMIST APPROACH

THERE ARE ENOUGH reasons to fear the possibility of a third world conflict. Currently, there is not a clear authority within the global order. It is not obvious the role international institutions should play in conflicts that pit powerful nations.

It is just a matter of time before the world knows another disastrous event in the liking of a World War. You might be asking what makes me so sure about the future of the world. I am not certain of the events to come. I hope this book does not project such an understanding. Still, there is a reality about the world, which we could ignore to our own existential demise.

When I look at a few events that happened in the past and compare them with incidents that are occurring today, all hints suggest that the possibilities for another, perhaps a much more devastating, world conflict are not that remote. There is a lot happening on the world stage. The problem is that there are fewer ways to deter unnecessary military buildups or senseless conflicts, be they regional or global. What is also clear is that most international institutions are inconsequential to a point where both State and non-State actors regularly act in complete impunity.

I reckon that this approach to the present international order might seem too alarmist. Others might say that it is a little bit over the top. Perhaps this take on world polity is unusual or even hyperbolic. To echo a previous point, there is a lot happening in the world. Many wars and conflicts are bourgeoning in various regions. We could not refute or even undermine many of these events.

It is true that no nation has formally declared its intent to enter an international conflict with the rest of the world. But one could speculate about such likelihood. It would also be naïve to presume that a major world conflict, which might pit certain nuclear powers against one another, would be impossible or even an absurd idea. If that were to happen, I am not sure that Western countries would consider Russia a friend (or an ally), just as it was the case during the Second World War[43]

Presently, the world is laden with conflicts. Some of these disagreements are domestic in nature. They often

---

[43] During both world wars (WWI and II), the Russian Empire (Soviet Union during WWI) was part of the international alliance against Hitler. Learn more by visiting these pages. The Editors of Encyclopaedia Britannica, "Allied Powers: International Alliance," Encyclopedia Britannica, accessed October 31, 2018, https://www.britannica.com/topic/Allied-Powers-international-alliance; Ishaan Tharoor, "Don't Forget How the Soviet Union Saved the World from Hitler," The Independent, May 9, 2016, http://www.independent.co.uk/news/world/the-soviet-union-helped-save-the-world-from-hitler-a7020926.html.

lead to tensions and even war. Other conflicts are between neighbor-countries who are incapable of finding amicable ways to resolve their differences.

Although many of these skirmishes are regional in nature, they have the potential to intensify to a larger quarrel. All across the globe, there are many clashes taking place, though they are not military in nature. We could sort many of these disagreements from serious to severe. We could consider the skirmish between Russia and Ukraine.

Within the last few years or so, Russia has conducted itself in ways that we could consider alarming for world peace. Its incursion in Crimea, for instance, is enough evidence to raise suspicion about the former Soviet Union's true objects in Eastern Europe. Fewer nations seem capable to stop Russia, at least when it comes to the country's search for regional dominance.

The rule of law also seems inconsequential for the Russians. Why is that the case? What is the extent of the rule of law in the world and not just in Eastern Europe? Let us explore further.

The Rule of Law

Is Russia a bellicose nation? Depending on whom you ask this question, the answer could be no. Certainly, Russia is a regional Hegemon both in and around Eastern Europe.

Russia is a major player in parts of Asia. Some analysts believe the Russian State may have a legitimate national security concern or even a relevant economic interest for seeking to set up some form of control over certain States in Eastern Europe. In any case, Russia has a place in the global order. The Russians are the only counterforce to the American supremacy.

Most people would argue that Russia is increasingly becoming an existential threat to various nations near or around the Russian-dominated region, notably for the countries that used to be part of the Soviet Union. The country's political leaders, mainly Vladimir Putin and Dmitry Medvedev, have been working exhaustingly to uphold a grip over those former territories.

Russian officials, on the other hand, might have a different approach in the debate. They might argue that when they intervene on other nation's territory or when they mangle in the political affairs of countries like Georgia or Ukraine, it is because they are pre-empting an existential threat from Western countries, including the United States and the United Kingdom. Seemingly, Russia sees itself under siege.

The Russian State has a deep fear of NATO.[44] Russian leaders oppose expanding this entity in Eastern Europe.[45] That fear, some might argue, could be irrational or immaterial, considering Russia's incontestable military superiority. Russian leaders view the presence of NATO in Eastern Europe "as aggressive and anti-Russian."[46]

---

[44] Ted Galen Carpenter, "Why Russia Fears NATO," Text, The National Interest, October 10, 2016, http://nationalinterest.org/blog/the-skeptics/why-russia-fears-nato-17999.

[45] Goldstein, *International Relations*, 90.

[46] Ibid.

Ted Carpenter argues that NATO is increasingly arrogant in Eastern Europe.[47] As a result, Russia seems unhappy about the true objects of Western powers in the region.[48] Let me echo that whether the previously stated views come from valid observations is not the concern of this work.

The "Cost-Benefit" of Obedience

The present arrangement of the international order is not conducive for nations to get what they want from other nations easily. A belligerent State could only achieve its goals through bullying means. Bullying could also have a disadvantage. When there is so much at stake, having a mass destructive arsenal of weaponry could be dangerous for world peace.

For most countries in Eastern Europe, Russia is a bully State. However, Russian leaders might not share a similar view. It is undeniable that Russia runs the risk of alienating itself on the international stage.

The country's leaders appear set in their pursuits in Eastern Europe. But the Americans seem determined to prevent that from happening. Therefore, the potential for a larger conflict between Russia and the United States is not an out of this world idea. The likelihood for a military skirmish between the Russian State and NATO or via third-party institutions is not that remote either.

---

[47] Carpenter, "Why Russia Fears NATO."

[48] Ibid.

The questions I am asking here is to what extent other nations should tolerate the bullying conducts of the Russian State. At which point such conducts could become alarming where they might threaten the existence of other nations both in and around Europe. The most alarming question to examine is the degree to which tries to tame Russia would be damaging to the region. We must also ask whether the countries that are closest to NATO would allow Russia to behave as if it owned them.

An important point of analysis, which might help us understand the nature of Russia's behavior in Eastern Europe, is the absence of the rule of law itself. At this point, Russia does not seem concerned for international institutions or the reach of IL itself. However, should it be that way? What could dissuade the Russians from misbehaving on the world stage?

We must explore the cleft between Russia and international institutions. We must explore the nature of IL. Let us review the foundation of this legal instrument.

Defining International Law

What does the term *"International Law"* entail? A simple way to put it is that this is the law of the international. This is the legal regime of the global order. Nonetheless, there is more to the term.

We often use the term IL to describe a body of laws that governs the conducts of sovereign States within the international order. Such laws often include rules, norms, and other standards of conducts. The question is who should enforce international legal principles. Currently, the

United Nations, for the most part, have the responsibility to enforce international laws.

The major problem with IL is its enforcement. International legal principles come from the notions that States are sovereign. Every State must recognize the sovereignty of other States. That is, States have a right to self-defense, both domestically and abroad (that is, on foreign territories). Each nation has a right to defend the self from external forces. Therefore, States enjoy some freedom, both the liberty to move about and the sovereignty to engage in commerce, which may include other dealings.

A crucial facet of IL worthy of note is the notion of consent. We cannot force States to obey agreements that they did not approve one way or another. The cornerstone of international legal principles is the understanding that States must enter some form of agreement with the international order. There are exceptions when it comes to abuses or violations about human rights. Under any circumstance, IL must apply to every nation.

The presumption is that international law or international-related agencies could serve as an antidote against *Rogue States*. However, the degree of the real power or the extent of the true influence international institutions, such as the UN, could leverage in conflicts like the one between Russia and Ukraine is still elusive. In the face of the mounting threat posed by the Russian State, international institutions appear increasingly irrelevant or excruciatingly powerless.

Several observers contended that IL could take effect when we need it the most. I, for one, disagree with that view. What is obvious is that over the last few decades, we could not use IL as effectively or as efficiently as we might have expected to deter outrageous conducts by Rogue Nations. IL has been incapable to stop self-absorb (that is, maniacal) leaders from getting their way in world affairs.

The effects of international rules and principles have not been significant enough to deter belligerent behaviors among Russian leaders. This could not be more obvious during the recent Ukraine debacle. International institutions have been unwilling (or incapable) to deter or even to slow down, a Vladimir Putin, whom, at first glance, wants to revive the old era of the Soviet Union.

The evidence suggests that Putin wants to reestablish a Russian dominion in the *Crimean Peninsula*. He did not hide his plan to retake Crimea. The evidence also shows that the international community stood by and did nothing. Therefore, they allowed Russia to conduct itself in ways that could be harmful to world peace.

Crimea is now a part of the Russian State. It will probably remain that way for a long time. The question worth asking here is what is it the international community could do to return Crimea to Ukraine. The answer is mute.

As of now, Crimea is a part of the Russian Federation. Any try to recapture the peninsula would trigger a regional conflict. The international community must precisely prevent just that. By that logic, Crimea is a lost case. What does that tell you about the influence of IL?

Other than a military action, fewer alternatives are available. So far, economic sanctions have yielded little or no tangible results on the behavior of the Russian State both in Eastern Europe and in other parts of the globe.

Then again, I must ask; what is the true nature of IL? What could this legal instrument do to prevent regional or world conflicts?

Let me echo that international rules of conducts often have little or no real effects in curbing the behaviors of some of the most belligerent leaders in the world. Perhaps this inability is by design. Perhaps this is the nature of the international order itself.

Part 3

A FLAWED LEGAL ORDER

CHAPTER 7

7. THE FLAWS OF INTERNATIONAL LAW

DO WE NEED a global leader? Although in principle, we could consider an international overseer as an important entity in the world. Such a presence might also undermine the notion that the world is chaos and anarchic. The inherent flaw in IL is the presupposition about its reach.

The ideals that led to creating IL overlooked the extent of its effectiveness without real results. There is a sense that IL could do no harm to certain institutions, for example when they act on behalf of a powerful State.

Arguably, IL, at least as a legal instrument, could be a useful legal tool. Nonetheless, only in a handful of cases former heads of States experienced legal prosecution. Even fewer of them faced the international judicial order either by a conviction or else under IL maxims. These instances, I would argue, are the exceptions. Targeted leaders often come from poor countries or countries that do not hold a significant seat at the international round table.

There exist fewer instances (or no instance at all) where former or current heads of States of powerful nations faced justice or punished any wrongdoings under IL maxims. This reality, I would echo, form the norms within the global order. For example, both during and after the Iraq war (2003-2008), many observers called for the international community to hold those responsible for the atrocities that took place in that part of the world accountable. They did nothing tangible.

Between 2008 and 2016, there had been spectacular deaths of innocent civilians caused by the abusive use of military drones in both Pakistan and Afghanistan. [49] As recently as 2018, there had been many casualties in Afghanistan itself. [50] Observers have called on the international community to intervene and to stop the drone madness. Most often, such demarches had been in futility.

Currently, there are no recourses available for those who suffer from the aggressive behavior of rogue actors. There are no other instances to enlist for help. Again, this is the nature of IL.

To this day, few people received sanctions or even fewer individuals have been tried for the human rights

---

[49] The Bureau of Investigative Journalism, "Drone Warfare," The Bureau of Investigative Journalism, accessed November 23, 2018, https://www.thebureauinvestigates.com/projects/drone-war.

[50] Jessica Purkiss and Abigail Fielding-Smith, "US Strikes Causing Civilian Casualties More than Double in Afghanistan," The Bureau of Investigative Journalism, October 11, 2018, https://www.thebureauinvestigates.com/stories/2018-10-11/us-strikes-causing-civilian-casualties-double.

abuses that took place in various parts of Iraq, Pakistan, and Afghanistan, just to name a few. In Egypt, for instance, the world overlooked, whether directly or implicitly, some of the most violent conducts against the people. Many in that part of the world must fend for themselves.

With the help of Western powers, a former military officer received a reward of presidential status after he oversaw a brutal crackdown[51] on dissidents against a coup, which ousted an elected president.[52] All of this occurred under the watchful eyes of the international community. How does that reflect on IL? What does that say about the rule of law?

---

[51] Human Rights Watch, "Egypt: Year of Abuses Under Al-Sisi," Human Rights Watch, June 8, 2015, https://www.hrw.org/news/2015/06/08/egypt-year-abuses-under-al-sisi; Samy Magdy, "Egypt's El-Sissi Begins 2nd Term amid Crackdown on Dissent," AP NEWS, June 2, 2018, https://apnews.com/30269d6316484d59a6227d893d49e1f9.

[52] Since the so-called "Arab Spring," Egypt is in a state of chaos. Although many were optimistic that the country would see a new era, a democratic era that is, little or no democracy has been found in that part of the world. The sad reality is that what has happened in Egypt transpired under the eyes of the international community. What is happening in Egypt is not secret. Yet, nothing had been done to stop the human rights abuses that are taking place in that country. See the following articles to learn more about Egypt. Jacob Wirtschafter, "Abdel-Fattah El-Sissi Cracks down on Dissent in Egypt," The Washington Times, November 15, 2018, https://www.washingtontimes.com/news/2018/nov/15/abdel-fattah-el-sissi-cracks-down-dissent-egypt/; Declan Walsh and Nour Youssef, "As Sisi Silences Critics, Hopes Fade That Egypt's Crackdown Will Ease," *The New York Times*, October 15, 2018, sec. World, https://www.nytimes.com/2018/05/23/world/middleeast/egypt-sisi-crackdown.html.

Meanwhile, the International Court is active in various parts of Latin America, Asia, and Africa. Indeed, the court held several leaders, many of whom were despotic at their core, accountable for their actions. Why is there a double standard?

Between 22 May 1947 and 1 August 2018, the International Court entered 175 cases in its general list.[53] Many more cases are in awaiting status. From 2018, at least seventeen cases are in waiting at the International Court of Justice. Many of these cases are common litigations.

The problem of IL is more vexing than the previously mentioned instances. Russia has proved the limits of IL and international institutions. That discount could not be more obvious in annexing Crimea. Ignoring IL is not just a Russian problem. As noted with Iraq, there is a more pervasive issue at play.

In addition, nations such as Iran, North Korea, Venezuela, and Syria, just to name a few of course, have conducted themselves in ways that highlighted inherent flaws in IL.[54] There are concerns that a potential alliance between Iran, Russia, and North Korea could be disastrous for world peace.[55] There are also concerns that Cuba and Venezuela could become a proxy for Rogue Nations such

---

[53] International Court of Justice, "Cases: International Court of Justice," accessed November 24, 2018, https://www.icj-cij.org/en/cases.

[54] Note that they often categorize these nations as belligerent states.

[55] Michael Ledeen, "Missiles and Menaces in an Iran-Russia-North Korea Alliance," Text, TheHill, February 13, 2015, http://thehill.com/blogs/pundits-blog/defense/232717-missiles-and-menaces-in-an-iran-russia-north-korea-alliance.

as North Korea and Iran to create problems in the Western Hemisphere.[56] These views reflect legitimate concerns, I would admit.

Most people consider these countries a threat to global peace and security. In 2010, Israeli Foreign Minister, Avigdor Lieberman, declared that Iran, Syria, and North Korea made up a "New 'Axis of Evil'" in the world.[57] Equally, most observers listed Israel as a belligerent State.

The endless feud between the State of Israel and the Palestinians fueled a big debate over the need for a stronger and a more effective international legal order. The actions posed by both Palestinian leaders and the Israelis have often shocked the world. Some observers accused the State of Israel of egregious violations of IL, chiefly when it comes to human rights. The government of Israel, on its end, always seems determined to undermine international legal principles, even in the face of irrefutable evidence of misconducts in Palestine or in other parts of the Middle Eastern region.

Many observers view Israel as a notorious violator of international rules. In many circles, one has a sense that the Israelis have little or no regards for the law. This reality could not be plainer when it comes to the country's growing disputes with Palestine.[58] Israel is a powerful

---

[56] Ibid.

The Associated Press, "Lieberman: Iran, Syria and North Korea Are New 'Axis of Evil,'" *Haaretz*, May 12, 2010, http://www.haaretz.com/israel-news/lieberman-iran-syria-and-north-korea-are-new-axis-of-evil-1.289866.

[58] Ireland Palestine Solidarity Campaign, "Israel's Violations of International Law: A Brief Introduction," Ireland Palestine Solidarity

nation. Just the same, Israel has powerful allies in the world, including the United States. What could they do to stop the State of Israel from ignoring IL? The answer is not clear.

What is plain is that many observers do not support Israel in its conduct in the Middle East. Even the United Nations called the Israel's occupation of Palestinian territories an act, which "Has no legal validity and constitutes a flagrant violation of international law."[59] This is also a viewpoint, which some observers have sought to refute or even undermine. Often, they have done so spectacularly.

Robert Stark, for instance, argues that the notion that Israel violated IL in Palestine is laughable. Israeli settlements are not a violation of IL, Stark further echoes.[60] The UN resolution, the author contends, is political in nature. Such a position, he retorts, is not binding under IL.[61]

The statement by Stark proves how much of a gag IL is in the eyes of so many people. He points out a few flaws in

---

Campaign, accessed July 9, 2017, http://www.ipsc.ie/israels-violations-of-international-law-a-brief-introduction.

[59] SC/12657 Security Council, "Israel's Settlements Have No Legal Validity, Constitute Flagrant Violation of International Law, Security Council Reaffirms, Meetings Coverage and Press Releases," December 23, 2016, https://www.un.org/press/en/2016/sc12657.doc.htm.

[60] Robert Stark, "Why Israeli Settlements Are Not a Violation of International Law," The Times of Israel, January 3, 2017, http://blogs.timesofisrael.com/why-israeli-settlements-are-not-a-violation-of-international-law/.

[61] Ibid.

the resolution, which I found intriguing, although I will not examine them here. This is the reality of IL. Its relevance and eventual application is always the subject of intense debates.

Without an effective enforcement tool or an apparatus, IL is going to remain an unpredictable exercise of legal maxims. Another reason to consider is that these legal principles are not always compatible with the long-term interests of powerful States. Thus, international legal principles are not always in line with the reality of the international order.

Relevance of International Law

Most powerful nation hold little or no regards for IL. Some consider the United States as one of those countries that undermine international rules, mainly when it suits them the most. Margot Patterson notes that even though the United States played a great role in creating international bodies, such as the League of Nations, the United Nations, the World Bank, the International Monetary Fund, and a litany of other global organizations, "when it comes to waging war, a cornerstone principle, more and more, the United States acts as if international law applies to other countries but not to itself."[62]

Shirley Scott, on her part, speaks of a dualism in her efforts to make sense of the way the United States is

---

[62] Margot Patterson, "How the U.S. Violates International Law in Plain Sight," America Magazine, October 12, 2016, https://www.americamagazine.org/politics-society/2016/10/12/how-us-violates-international-law-plain-sight.

committed to IL. [63] This well-known scholar in international affairs notes that the United States is ambivalent about what is seeks from IL. The author outlines a contradiction in the way the American government has treated international legal principles. According to Scott, we could sum up that inconsistency in the following manner:

"Between stated intentions and real-world results, between what the United States says about an international rule of law and what it does in specific scenarios; between what the United States seems to think others should do and what it does itself; between US acceptance of international economic law as compared with its seemingly lower regard for certain other fields; between its promotion of the principle of sovereign equality and US Exceptionalism; and between US engagement at different points in time."[64]

The preceding understanding sums up the United States stance in most legal issues globally. Russia has espoused a similar slant about IL (or international principles). The previous quote also suggests that we could not deter countries like the United States, North Korea, Iran, Israel, and Russia in their pursuit, whether legitimate or else, simply by a mere threat of sanctions. The reality is

---

[63] Shirley V. Scott, *International Law, US Power: The United States' Quest for Legal Security*, 1 edition (Cambridge: Cambridge University Press, 2012), 2.

[64] Ibid.

that this is as far as IL could go (at least often) when it comes to enforcement.

Because of the way certain nations have treated international rules, it can be difficult for them to impose any glare of moral superiority to other States. This understanding gave Russia an edge during the Ukraine debacle. The Russian State enjoys the status of an important player within the international order. Russia knows the rules and understands the extent to which they apply. Because of its status at the UN, Russia knows and understands the reality of the council.

Inciting Misbehaviors

As echoed in previous parts, the most pressing limit of IL is its application or enforcement. Ipso facto, international laws do not apply universally. This reality brings to evidence a much more serious issue. That is, why we need IL in the first place? When does it applies and to whom it should apply.

To deter a powerful nation like Russia from indexing the part of a sovereign State like Ukraine, a threat of military action would have been the most fitting. This formula worked in 1991 when Iraq, under the leadership of Saddam Hussein, invaded Kuwait.[65] The defeat that the Iraqi military suffered at the time—in what we know now

---

[65] See the United States Office of the Historian to learn more about the first Gulf War. United States Department of State Office of the Historian, Bureau of Public Affairs, "The First Gulf War, Short History," Department History, Office of the Historian, accessed July 9, 2017, https://history.state.gov/departmenthistory/short-history/firstgulf.

as the first Gulf War—was considerable. It forced Saddam Hussein to make an about-face in Kuwait. Is this a fair analogy?

Granted, there is a world of a difference between Russia and Iraq. For example, Russia is a much more powerful nation. The Russian army is among the best military machines in the world. Russia also has a long history of standing its ground. In this case, Russia would be a formidable foe. The world knows that.

Few countries would make an empty military threat to the Russian State, knowing that Russian leaders might call their bluff. Russia is a nuclear nation. The Russian State has a strong army, which could reply with an equal (or a greater) force to any attack. The Russian armed forces could face any military machine in the world.

Considering the previously stated explanations, one could make the case that Russia is untamable. As a result, Russia has the flexibility to act in complete impunity. Some observers have argued this is precisely the reason Russia has been misbehaving on the world stage.

Preemption versus Prevention

In principle, international legal doctrines come from the notion of prevention. Such an instrument came about as a preventive apparatus within the international order. But history also showed that they often used international legal methods preemptively.

If a powerful nation wants to evoke the law as a reason to violate the rights, which international groups have a duty to protect, the common path is to get a UN resolution, which would provide a legal rationale (or a legal outline) to do or to omit from doing. The problem is that the UN, at least as an institution, is not as neutral as one would think.

As already echoed, nations that happen to hold a powerful position within this international body often decide its course of action. Powerful members can influence (often, they have done so in a slight for human rights) international bodies to implement international laws that regularly favor their own interests. They know how to manipulate that entity to get what they want from it. They know how and to undermine what they do not want from it.

For many observers, it is almost impossible to remove politics or political ideologies in the actions taken by the UN. The belief is that every resolution adopted by the UN is political at its core. Every UN action could be to the benefit of one country or for several nations. Such an act could also be to the harm of one country or several nations.

This presumption of neutrality makes the UN a fragile institution. There is no way around that. This is the nature of the UN itself.

The law must be a buffer, which could prevent self-interests and other nationalistic ideals from taking over this international institution. In theory, every action adopted at the UN must reflect a common agreement, which is in turn the result of the laws agreed on by the members of the institution. But the reality can be a bit different. The UN is not (or could never be) a neutral arbiter. The law must be the compass, which would guide this institution. The problem is that this is seldom the case, at least not in practical terms. There lies the issue of acuity, I would argue.

The legal bearings of a UN resolution (at times their moral merit) can be questionable. Sometimes, they create passionate, if not fierce, debates. Many are [66] quick to rebuke UN actions, which point out a state's misconduct within the international order. This approach to refute international initiatives spearheaded by the UN holds the signature of the State of Israel.

Supporters of Israel rejected almost every UN actions against the country's affiliation with Palestine. Granted, it would not be fair to classify Israel as the only State that seems determined to undermine international rule of law in every way possible. Israel is not alone in its aim to undermine IL at every stage of its application.

Other belligerent nations are often reluctant to recognize the authority of international institutions. They are likely to undermine the UN Security Council. Sometimes, they do so to weaken the rule of law itself. Here, Iran is the best example that comes to mind. The continent of Africa also has authoritarian regimes that echo similar viewpoints. Asia has its share of leaders who seem determined to undermine the rule of law. In it lies the issue.

Many view the entity that must uphold international principles independent. Observers often put in question the authority of the UN either to commit or to omit a particular conduct by its own members. To echo a previous

---

[66] They also have the common appellation of microstates.

analysis, this is the nature of the debate about the scope of the rule of law at the international level. I would argue that IL is weak; more often than not, it is inconsequential in world polity.

They often use international legal principles as an offensive strategy. They habitually used them as a legal frame for preemptive military actions. The UN has its own armed forces or law enforcement machine, which many know as peacekeeping institutions. Nonetheless, these units are military in nature.[67] By relying on that understanding, we could also consider IL a brutal medium, which could induce conflicts.

The presence of certain international institutions must prevent States from going rogue. International law must deter a State like Israel (or even Russia) from engaging in certain misconducts. The Russian State seems unaffected by those bodies.

Russia regularly engages in many of the conducts, which international institutions have a duty to contain. If the goal were peace, the result of any demarche to achieve that peace would always be war. If the goal were war, the best apparatus to achieve such a goal would be through IL.

---

[67] The United Nations has its own Peacekeeping forces, which has the mission of helping counties torn by conflicts to have peace. It is a force of approximately 110,000 active personnel. Their goal is help countries negotiate the "difficult path from conflict to peace." To learn more, please visit the UN peacekeeping website. United Nations Peacekeeping, "United Nations Peacekeeping," United Nations Peacekeeping, accessed November 27, 2018, https://peacekeeping.un.org/en/node.

There exists fewer means to stop powerful nations from going rogue. Thus, we live in a world of controlled chaos.

The notion of international law, in its present form, offers belligerent nations the legal model to act in total impunity. Presently, international legal barriers, I would say, constrain other nations from defending themselves against institutions that are more powerful (economically, politically, or militarily) than they are. Powerful international bodies often enjoy a large control over international norms and rules.

A double standard about IL is worth pointing out here as well. Smaller European States like Andorra, Liechtenstein, Malta, Monaco, and San Marino, just to name a few, could not envisage a military incursion in any other States without huge economic, political, and military effects. To these States, IL could make a difference. Perhaps this was Saddam Hussein's biggest mistake in 1991.[68]

For some powerful States, the reality is much more complex. For countries like Russia, United Kingdom, Australia, Israel, and France, IL is irrelevant. In this case, this is just to name a few. But these countries are likely to undermine IL when their interests are at stake. IL could be a cause in leading to wars, rather than upholding peace. I would refer to IL as an impulsive legal tool, which does not serve the international order.

---

[68] See CNN facts about the war to learn more. CNN Library, "Gulf War Fast Facts," CNN, August 2, 2016, http://www.cnn.com/2013/09/15/world/meast/gulf-war-fast-facts/index.html.

CHAPTER 8

8. WESTERN POWERS AND UKRAINE

THE STATE OF UKRAINE has been in the news. A nation that once stood as part of the Russian empire, was struggling to hold its sovereignty in the face of what many considered a Russian-driven domestic turmoil. The question in the minds of most people was whether international institutions, such as the UN, should (or could) play a prominent role in the crisis.

The United States appeared set in its position against Russia's actions in the region. The Americans and their allies, namely Great Britain, and France seemed settled on preventing Russia from overpowering other States, notably in Eastern Europe. One had a sense that a *laissez-frapper* (let it hit) between Russia and NATO was imminent.

Some nations sought a diplomatic compromise against Russia. The Americans spearheaded several international efforts on this issue. Several nations condemned Russia's aggression in Ukraine. Unlike the United States, however, many of these nations took little or no immediate sanctions against the Russian State.

The question worth asking is why Russia had been acting so belligerently. What is the reason fewer nations openly condemned Russia's actions in Ukraine? Why the United States, at least under President Barack Obama, had been so outspoken against the Russians? The crisis in Ukraine offers the opportunity to assess why IL is an important legal tool.

Examining the Crisis in Ukraine

Between 2013 and 2015, the world witnessed several terrible events, which had been taking place in Ukraine. Many heads turned toward international institutions, such as the UN or NATO, to step-in. Their demands were clear; they wanted the UN to find a way to resolve the crisis.

The *Internet* has many opinion pieces, blog posts, and videos about the events that dominated the conversation in Ukraine. From November 2018, the world has forgotten the crisis in Ukraine. The country is not always in the news. This is shocking, considering the issues in Ukraine are still growing.

So far, the conflict in Eastern parts of the country has claimed more than 10,000 lives.[69] "Ukraine is still on the

---

[69] Samantha Raphelson, "'Simmering Conflict' In Eastern Ukraine Remains At An Impasse," NPR.org, January 10, 2018, https://www.npr.org/2018/01/10/577104670/simmering-conflict-in-eastern-ukraine-remains-at-an-impasse.

edge," echoed Stefan Wolff and Tatyana Malyarenko.[70] Various parts of the country are experiencing humanitarian crises. Donbas is among the worst humanitarian crises in the world.[71] The crisis in Ukraine is more complex than most people realize.[72]

The presumption, at least in most Western media, is that everything is fine in Ukraine. Until now, Crimea is still part of Russia. This new reality suggests an implicit acceptance among the international community of what took place in that part of the region.

Another issue to consider is that the inaction against Russia suggests world leaders' incapacity to contain the Russian State itself. Just a few years ago, there was a sense of urgency to sanction Russia. There was a global outcry against the country. Now, there is a more conciliatory tone.

What changed during that time? Seemingly, nothing changed on the ground. Nonetheless, the political tone within the international community has died down.

---

[70] Stefan Wolff is Professor of International Security, University of Birmingham. Tatyana Malyarenko Professor of International Relations, National University Odesa Law Academy. See their piece at: Stefan Wolff and Tatyana Malyarenko, "Ukraine Is Still on the Edge, despite All Efforts to Stabilise It," The Conversation, accessed November 24, 2018, http://theconversation.com/ukraine-is-still-on-the-edge-despite-all-efforts-to-stabilise-it-92004.

[71] Cynthia Buckley et al., "The War in Ukraine Is More Devastating than You Know," Washington Post, April 9, 2018, https://www.washingtonpost.com/news/monkey-cage/wp/2018/04/09/the-war-in-ukraine-is-more-devastating-than-you-know/.

[72] Ibid.

What led to the public reaction against Russia? What did Russia do that other nations found so unpleasant? The answer may be hard to pin down.

Russia's action in Crimea was not a novel act within the international system. Other nations engaged in similar conducts. But it is probable that a well-orchestrated machine sought to smear the Russian State for the same behaviors that many powerful States overlooked in the past.

Perhaps the reason Ukraine received such media scrutiny was because its problems also came about because of external forces other than Russia itself. The Russian State increasingly asserted itself, some might say menacingly, in Eastern Europe. That militant attitude among Russia posed a serious problem for many Western powers. Anyway, it would be naïve to ignore the role of these powers in the Ukrainian debacle.

Most of the outcry against Russia was not necessarily about Ukraine itself. Some might argue that it was about the power struggle between Russia and powerful institutions, such as the United States and Great Britain. Ukraine was a victim. Crimea found itself caught up in the middle of a nasty feud between Vladimir Putin and Western oligarchs. During the unfolding in Ukraine, IL was powerless to contain the incident.

Assumptions about the Power of the Law

A few presumptions about IL are worth pointing out here. International legal doctrines presume the existence of an important legal tool, which not only oversees world events, but also creates instruments or tools that could restrict

State conduct. The goal of this legal means, most people presume, is to prevent certain States from engaging in aggressive behaviors. The popular assumption is that we could understand the world unitarily. Nonetheless, the crisis in Ukraine revealed some of the most poignant flaws in this approach to world affairs.

Another common belief is that State (or non-state) actors could be accountable for their actions. They should also be responsible for their omissions in certain circumstances when it comes to human rights violations and other domestic atrocities. This utopian view of the world could be obvious in the way they designed international institutions. The goal of these global institutions is to aim for an eventual world order.

Although few made this point directly, the primary goal of IL is perhaps the results of a want to achieve global peace. The idea is that grandiose universal sets of legal principles could guide State conducts both internationally and domestically. But that is not always the case.

In practice, few think that IL could make a difference in world affairs. Many observers put in question the authority of the institutions that created it. To reiterate, the United States is one of the instigators of IL. However, it does not afford much relevance to this body. The American government often refutes IL, especially when it does not suit their interests both domestically and internationally.

They designed laws specifically to regulate behaviors between nations. We could also classify such laws as an inaccurate approach to the international order itself. The presupposition is that IL, as a field of law, provides an outline for scholars and practitioners alike to understand the law of the international and to assess the international order. The problem is that there is a dearth of consensus about the true effect of international legal principles to redress the world's most pressing problems.

When it comes to how IL works, when it comes to how IL applies, or when it comes to why we should evoke international legal principles to explain real world issues, there is no consensus. This facet of the debate remains a contentious undertaken. It is often the results of ideologies or mistaken ideas about the world. This is perhaps the reason international institutions enjoy little or no tangible influence on powerful nations. Let us examine the origins of the authority that guides international legal principles.

Limits of Authority

In most political corridors, there is little sympathy for Russia. Few Western leaders would openly support the Russian State's aggression against Ukraine. Others reject the country's behaviors in other parts of Eastern Europe.

In most academic circles, some observers view Russia as an agglomeration of villains and corrupt politicians. While I do not delve in this facet of the debate, it is important to examine the conducts of the Russian State under a microscope. It is necessary to assess the issue of enforcement with more interest, with forethought, in trying to understanding how international agreements could foster peace. It is essential to examine the limits of IL. There is also a need to explore the degree to which powerful nations obey international rules and principles.

We must assess flaws in the enforcement article of IL. There is also a need to relay the degree to which international agencies can be inconsequential, circumspectly when the perpetrators are among the nations that must enforce the law itself. What might explain the nature of the belligerent attitude the Russian State consistently adopt in world affairs?

Russia is a powerful member of the UN Security Council. It plays a great role in the decisions taken by that entity. It is important to understand the role this international body plays in taming the Russian State. There is a need to examine IL in practice.

CHAPTER 9

9. RELEVANCE OF INTERNATIONAL LAW

THE FOUNDATION OF international legal principles is sound. Its application, however, is still in infancy. That reality makes IL seems irrelevant. This is the case when it comes to its enforcement. The role of the international community in the most striking issues affecting the world remains dubious.

This subject of law is laden with distorted assumptions about the world and the objects of powerful actors. Notions supporting IL contain mistaken expectations about how such a legal approach may affect State relations. There are misgivings about the extent of the conducts of powerful States on the world stage. This legal instrument, I would further note, is more theoretical than it is practical.

Common understandings about the extent of IL (or views) about the nature of international issues are often incongruent, when it comes to theory and practice. The understanding itself makes sense. There is a need for a legal order. There is also a need to police the conducts of every State within the international community.

The same legal order that applies domestically should apply also internationally. Domestically, laws govern the members of a particular social setting. The question is why that would be different for nations that interact within the international order. There should not be any exception. I reckon that in practice, there is a clear difference.

In theory, there is a need for IL. The use of such a legal tool would make sense in a world of confusion. The reason worth pointing out is the notion of chaos. Most people understand that we live in a world of anarchy.[73] At this point, IL seems unfeasible or even impracticable. Why is there such a barrier to developing IL?

Just like most domestic laws, IL comes from sound legal models. This facet of law reflects indisputable legal ideas. The problem is that observers seldom view international legal principles from a universal prism.

International principles are rarely enforceable. A few reasons could account for that. The power of international institutions is relative. That is, the reach of such powers often depends on the size, the economic status, the military capacities, or the willingness of individual States to obey international rules.

When a powerful State violates international norms, by default, international institutions can do little or nothing to sanction that State. As a result, the extent to which IL

---

[73] Amos A. Jordan et al., *American National Security* (JHU Press, 2009). Jordan et al. (2009) defines anarchy as a lack of formal and authoritative government.

could have an independent effect on State behavior remains an open-ended question. Nonetheless, it is important to assess the impetus of IL. Even so, we must do so within the context of State behavior. We must also revisit Russia's annexation of Crimea to understand the reach of IL.

While many on the world stage vigorously condemned this act, Russia has yet to receive an enough punishment. This proves that IL, in its current form, is only relative.[74] One could best understand it in context. It offers little or no incentive for States to stop from conducts that violate international norms. For most nations, there are no real results for misbehaving on the world stage.

Lack of a Legal Model

Before I delve in the legal implications of Russia's actions in Crimea, let us stroll back through the hills of history. There is a need to understand what sets up the legal underpinnings of IL. We could explore this facet of IL from two angles (that is, a short and a long approach).

The long approach would elaborate on the origin of this field of law. Most scholars would contend that IL

---

[74] By contextual, I mean that every crisis is different. As a result, state behavior may vary depending of the problem. It may be in the interest of a state like Russia to abide by International Law when it comes to international trade agreements. However, Russia may be reluctant to uphold International Law in border disputes. In the case of Crimea, Russia's legal stance seemed to rest on the notion that it has a responsibility to protect Russian-speaking dissidents in Crimea. From their standpoint, that protection requires the violation of the territorial integrity of another nation.

stemmed from several legal ideas, including natural and positive law. I would not necessarily object to this viewpoint.

The short approach would help us assess the truth of IL, at least as a separate field of law. Nonetheless, I must point out that IL, in and of itself, is not a field of law. Rather, it is a disjointed compilation of do's and don'ts in the international order. I must say that the extent to which behaviors internationally reflects a larger idea, which many regard highly (or widely accept), remains unclear.

One of the major traits of any law is obedience. Every law must create some form of obedience. An effective law must create an obligation to obey.

Many echoed a similar argument in the literature about legal theory. When it comes to the realistic facet of IL, obedience is depressingly optional. That is the reason enforcing international legal maxims can be selective.

John Austin, a renowned legal positivist, argues that command is ideal to create obligation in the law.[75] Such a command must come from a particular authority. There is not such a back-and-forth within the international order. No one country dominates the world.[76]

---

[75] John Austin, *Austin: The Province of Jurisprudence Determined*, ed. Wilfrid E. Rumble, 1st edition (Cambridge; New York, NY: Cambridge University Press, 1995).

[76] The understanding is that the United States dominates the world. As a result, since the fall of the Soviet Union, the United States is the sole power in world politics. The understanding is that the cold war has led to unipolarity. (See Richard Spielman, "The Emerging Unipolar World," *The New York Times*, August 21, 1990, sec. Opinion, https://www.nytimes.com/1990/08/21/opinion/the-emerging-unipolar-world.html. Of course, this has never been the case in reality.

Even in a unipolar order, there is not a primary authority. [77] The notion of unipolarity symbolizes the degree to which one country could impose its will in world polity. That imposition does not necessarily involve obedience. Thus, obedience to international norms (or rules) is about the power difference between the entity that seeks to enforce such norms or such rules.

Obedience as a Calculated Choice

The international order is empty of a formal rule and any form of an authoritative government.[78] It is true that the laws are there. Their applications are context-specific.

We could make out obedience to international rules as a calculated choice, which State actors make by relegating their predicaments within the stratum of world affairs. That calculation often entails an assessment of their military capacities and economic power. That obedience is

---

Nonetheless, the common belief is that we live in a unipolar world. (See Eirik B. Lundestad and Tor G. Jakobsen, "A Unipolar World: Systems and Wars in Three Different Military Eras," *POPULAR SOCIAL SCIENCE* (blog), February 5, 2013, http://www.popularsocialscience.com/2013/02/05/a-unipolar-world-systems-and-wars-in-three-different-military-eras/.

[77] The concept of polarity is very common in international relations. It is the understanding that one State dominates the distribution of power within the international system. One state controls every aspect of the world, including in terms of culture, economy, and military. See Wikipedia, "Polarity (International Relations)," *Wikipedia*, October 2, 2018, https://en.wikipedia.org/w/index.php?title=Polarity_(international_rel ations)&oldid=862212102.

[78] Jordan et al., *American National Security*.

short-lived so long as the nation in question does not have the means to retaliate against the nation that seeks its obedience from a particular law or legal principle.

Perhaps this is the reason many nations, including Iran and North Korea, seek nuclear abilities. Perhaps it is a form of existential assurance (or it is a form of protection) from the threat posed by other nations. It might also be the reason belligerent nations do not wish to see certain nations own nuclear weaponry. Within the international order, obedience is not the result of mutual respect of existing laws.

Obedience can be about military powers or a country's willingness to obey the rules set forth by others. Most nations want to be the ones who set the rules. Therefore, there is always a power struggle to dominate the international order.

The previous reality makes it indispensable for smaller countries or least influential nations to obey international rules. It also makes it almost impossible to force powerful nations to uphold those laws. In it stems the contentious nature of IL, above all, as a source of authority in the world or as the foundation of commands.

Since IL creates little or no real obligation to obey, there can be little or no real enforcement apparatus, which could deter a State actor from engaging in mischievous conducts. That reality also affords non-State actors the leeway to act in complete impunity in certain regions. For that reason, the line between governmental and non-governmental actions is blurry.

The American Central Intelligence Agency (also known as the CIA) is notorious for engaging in conducts overseas, which some could consider a violation of international norms.[79] Yet, this agency often acts outside the scope of international principles. Then, what is the extent of IL for non-State actors, especially when they act for a particular State? Presently, the answer is not clear.

What is evident is that international legal principles do not apply under similar circumstances, even though non-State actors could have an important influence on a particular State. Therefore, one could suppose that IL does not have an "independent" effect on the behavior of States or non-State actors. This reality was obvious in Ukraine in 2014.

Russia showed no reverence for international norms during the crisis. It was not the first time that Russia adopted such a stance in the region though. In 2008, a similar episode played out in Georgia. From here, let us examine the Ukraine incident a bit closer to make sense of it all.

A Powerless Ukraine

In 2013, Ukraine descended in complete anarchy. During that time, the Russian State had been in the news; it was not for good reasons. There was a constant political unrest in Ukraine. Many parts of the country experienced panic.[80] For a while, the skirmishes died down.

---

[79] The CIA (Central Intelligence Agency) and other secretive agencies often operate outside the purview of international rules and principles.

[80] The anti-government protest in Ukraine gained momentum in 2014 when many Ukrainian dissidents demanded the departure of President Viktor Yannukovich.

Between November and December 2013, Ukraine slowly, but surely, descended into chaos. Some observers labeled this moment *"The Euromaidan Protest."*[81] Thousands of protesters and the police clashed on the streets of Kiev. Many protesters wanted Ukraine's government to reverse course and sign a landmark agreement with the European Union in defiance of Russia.[82] Many sought to end Russia's *main-mise* on their government. The Ukrainian government resisted.

I saw the police crackdown on the *Internet.* I listened to political pundits on major new outlets. I also saw the conflict worsened in what Nick Thompson (from CNN) called "The bloodiest conflict in Europe since the wars over the former Yugoslavia in the early 1990s."[83] Yet, every hint signaled that international institutions were powerless to change the course of the events in Ukraine. I foresaw that the incident would unfold precisely the way Russia wanted.

---

[81] It was a series of protests in Kiev's Maidan Nezalezhnosti (Independence Square). To learn more, see David R. Marples, "Euromaidan and the Conflict in Ukraine in 2013–14," Encyclopedia Britannica, December 29, 2014, https://www.britannica.com/topic/Euromaidan-and-the-Conflict-in-Ukraine-in-2013-14-2006898.

[82] Annys Shin, "Recalling the 2013 Protests in Ukraine," Washington Post, accessed November 21, 2018, https://www.washingtonpost.com/lifestyle/magazine/recalling-the-2013-protests-in-ukraine/2017/11/13/f9a8ba90-ae89-11e7-be94-fabb0f1e9ffb_story.html.

[83] Nick Thompson, "Ukraine: Everything You Need to Know about How We Got Here," CNN, February 3, 2017, https://edition.cnn.com/2015/02/10/europe/ukraine-war-how-we-got-here/index.html.

Many Ukrainians accused President Viktor Yannukovich of being a corrupt leader. Dissidents also denounced the President's tendency to allow Russia to meddle in Ukrainian affairs. The pressure of the streets mounted to a point where it eventually led to the ouster of president Yannukovich.

Many political analysts argued that what happened in Ukraine was not a spontaneous movement. There were some powerful forces behind what seemed like a movement of the people and by the people. The argument was that Western powers played a role in Yannukovich's ouster. That view resounded in the streets of Moscow. In the halls of the Russian government, there was a sense of urgency to regain control of Ukraine.

In most Western media outlets as well, there were diverging views about the nature of what was occurring in Ukraine. What was obvious to most observers is that the absence of President Yannukovich created a power vacuum in the country. For a while, there was an atmosphere of ambiguity about who was acting on whom to do what and for what purpose. This political reality, some might say, provided Russia the pretext it needed to interject itself in Ukraine.

To the astute observer, it seemed evident that the political misgivings that embroiled Ukraine allowed Russia to play a larger role in the country's internal polity. Amid the societal dysfunction that engulfed Ukraine, there was a sense that further turmoil was around the corner. Sentiments against the Russian State grew rapidly. There was a sense that the lives of individuals with Russian origins were in imminent danger. At that point, Russia poised itself as the savior of the Russian-speaking population in Ukraine.

Russia exploited this moment of political doubt in Ukraine to instill more chaos in the country. Soon thereafter, Russia took over the Ukrainian State, at least parts of it. The political upheaval opened the door for the Russian military to take a position in Crimea.

Russia claimed that it needed to protect the Russian-speaking population in certain parts of the region. Then, the Russian State, under Vladimir Putin's leadership, annexed Crimea. This part of the region has historically been a prize, which Russian officials always sought to reclaim.

Crimea held a referendum over the need to join Russia. The results were unanimous. Most Crimean residents wanted to join Russia. On the other hand, the international community rejected the results of the referendum. Most world powers called the referendum a sham. Still, that did not stop Crimea from becoming a part of the Russian Federation.[84]

The effects of the Russian annexation were real across Ukraine. The idea that we could detach Crimea from the Ukrainian State echoed throughout the country. Other regions wanted to vote in favor of secession from Ukraine. Separatist movements had sprout in various parts of the country, including in Donetsk and Kharkiv.

Other States feared that Russia might attempt to take control of their region. There was a genuine apprehension

---

[84] After the Ukrainian President, Viktor Yannukovich, left the country, Russia sent soldiers and took control of the Crimea region.

that Russia might try to regain control of some of the States, which declared their independence after the fall of the Soviet Union. Of course, most Western powers wanted to prevent such a fate.

Short of engaging Russia on the military front, what alternatives Western powers had against the Russian military might? Perhaps no viable (or perhaps no tenable) options, I would say. If that were Russia's true intent, what (or who) could have stopped the Russian State? I will let you be the judge of that.

Arguably, this is where the issue can be a bit complicated. This is where applying IL could have made a huge difference. Let us explore the Ukrainian crisis further.

Part 4

THE DRAWBACKS

CHAPTER 10

10. CONTAINING VLADIMIR PUTIN

AS I SOUGHT TO prove in this book thus far, Russia is on the rise as a global power. Under Vladimir Putin, one of the country's most powerful heads of state, Russia has become a growing threat in Eastern Europe. Many heads of States fear the Russian State. The question is what they could do to contain Russia. What could they do to contain Vladimir Putin? At this point, answers are not clear.

The only tool the international community has at its disposal against Russia is enforcing the rule of law. Such enforcement must take place at the demand of the United Nations Security Council. That enforcement must be for instilling peace in the world. The problem is that Russia is also a member of the council. Russia has veto power in what the council does or does not do.

Since Russia has a major role in the international order, Russian leaders could affect any measures against their state. Perhaps this was the reason Russia could frame the debate about its presence in Crimea as a national issue.

The view was that the Russian-speaking population was vulnerable to human rights violations in Ukraine. It was up to Russia to protect these people. From the Russian's vantage point, any actions the Russian State undertook in Crimea were by it righteous.

The previous viewpoint is not a solid argument. Nonetheless, some might argue that it is a legitimate claim. Russia and Ukraine have a long history. The two countries had a fierce conflict over the Crimean peninsula, which was part of Russia, but became part of Ukraine since the 1950s.[85]

Ukraine was once a vibrant part of the Russian empire. However, since the collapse of the Soviet Union, Russia recognized Ukraine as an independent State. Russian officials recognized Ukraine's present borders. [86] Russia signed various treaties with Ukraine, some of which are bilateral and clearly state that the Russian State should stop itself from aggression or warfare against Ukraine.

In 1994, both countries agreed on a political arrangement, which would guarantee the territorial integrity (or the political independence) of Ukraine. This agreement came about within the context of the Memorandum 51, [87]which the United Kingdom, Russia, and the United States

---

[85] Goldstein, *International Relations*, 180.

[86] Marc Weller, "Analysis: Why Russia's Crimea Move Fails Legal Test," BBC News, accessed September 4, 2015, http://www.bbc.com/news/world-europe-26481423.

[87] Russia and Ukraine signed the Budapest memorandum in 1994; it guaranteed the security of Ukraine in exchange for removing nuclear weapons from its territory (Marc Weller).

signed. The agreement provided security assurances against threats (or use of force) among the co-signed nations.

In 1997, Russia signed a two-way treaty, a Partition Treaty as it were, with Ukraine, which settled the status and the conditions of the Black Sea Fleet. This treaty stipulated that both Russia and Ukraine have a stake in the Crimean Peninsula. In 2014, perhaps before annexing Crimea, Russia one-sidedly withdrew from the treaty. In it lies the crux of the issues between Russia and Ukraine.

There is always a way around international legal principles. Belligerent leaders know how to take advantages of these loopholes. This is the essence of IL, to echo here.

The Legal Issues

It is incontestable that Russia is unpredictable within the international order. A few issues are worth examining further. It is important to explore the legal issues that permeate IL. The laws are not clear about what is the best course of action against the Russian State when it misbehaves on the world stage.

No one knows what will be the country's next move. As already stipulated, there is much apathy toward Russia In most Western countries. The Russian State's recent incursion in Ukraine has led many Western observers to question Russian leaders' true intents.

Few people could defend Russia's actions in Ukraine. But does that mean that Russia could be a threat to international peace? There is confusion there. Regionally, the consensus is that Russia is a menace for long-term peace in Eastern Europe.

In all fairness, I must further note that the Russian
State has not been hostile to only Ukraine. In the past,
Russia experienced a few skirmishes with its neighbors.
Ukraine is the latest Russian brawl in a series of incidents,
which many observers considered as the country's most
aggressive conducts toward its closest neighbors yet.

Within the last few years or so, Russia has shown its
ugly side to the world. So far, there had not been any
suitable answer to the country's actions. Instead, the world
responded by smearing Russian leaders, markedly Vladimir
Putin. Is that a winning strategy? Some might say no. Here,
I would agree.

On Western media outlets, Russia is constantly in the
news. They are likely to parade the country as a lawless
nation. They regularly portray Vladimir Putin as the world's
most menacing villain. The former Secretary of State under
President Barack Obama (2009-2013) and presidential
candidate (2016), Hillary Clinton, compared President
Putin with Adolf Hitler.[88] While these epithets have not
deterred Putin in his searches, they have surely
strengthened his uncompromised views on certain issues,

---

[88] Associated Press, "Hillary Clinton Says Vladimir Putin's Crimea
Occupation Echoes Hitler," *The Guardian*, March 6, 2014, sec. World
news, https://www.theguardian.com/world/2014/mar/06/hillary-
clinton-says-vladimir-putins-crimea-occupation-echoes-hitler; What in
the world? Pieces of global opinion BBC News, "Hillary Clinton's
Putin-Hitler Analogy," March 6, 2014, sec. Echo Chambers,
https://www.bbc.com/news/blogs-echochambers-26476643.
Certainly, Mrs. Clinton tried to explain the context of her criticism of
President Putin. See CNN, *Hillary Clinton On Putin-Hitler Comment*,
2016, https://www.youtube.com/watch?v=ZixsVwcofEw.

including the conflict in Syria. Certainly, many observers condemned the Putin-Hitler analogy.[89]

In certain Western regions, one could hardly defend the Russian State without experiencing a smearing campaign. Russia has a long record of engaging in behaviors. This conduct is out of line with Western expectations. The degree to which demonizing Vladimir Putin or his allies would halt the Russian State in its search for regional dominance is unrealistic.

Indeed, Russia engaged in a series of behaviors, which we could construe as provocative, if not flat out aggressive. Arguably, these actions have not been conducive to regional peace. They do not incite security both from a regional and globally. This is the trademark of the Russian State itself.

Russia has always been practical. The country has a long record of mingling in the affairs of other nations, prominently in countries that once made up the Soviet Union. Russian foreign approach is notorious for interfering in regional politics. The notion that we could tame Russia's influence in Eastern Europe (or in the world) is unrealistic.

We could argue that whether Vladimir Putin is in power, Russia will still be Russia.[90] Smearing the Russian

---

[89] Philip Rucker, "Hillary Clinton's Putin-Hitler Comments Draw Rebukes as She Wades into Ukraine Conflict," *The Washington Post*, March 5, 2014, http://www.washingtonpost.com/politics/hillary-clintons-putin-hitler-comments-draw-rebukes-as-she-wades-into-ukraine-conflict/2014/03/05/31a748d8-a486-11e3-84d4-e59b1709222c_story.html.

State or its leaders would probably strengthen the country's belligerent stance in world polity. There ought to be a more productive approach, if not a practical stance, to the Russian problem. This is where IL could play a significant role. It could contain the rise of Russia in world politics.

Powerful nations have undermined IL to a point where they themselves could not enforce it. They could not do so even when it would matter the most. According to the rule of law, Russia would have had little or no excuse to annex Crimea. Therefore, Ukraine would have had a legitimate course of actions against the Russian State for its aggression. But this is not what took place.

In the end, Russia annexed Crimea. Shockingly, Russian leaders (their allies as well) suffered little or no tangible results. Sanctions, be they economic or else, have had little or no immediate effects on the Russian State.

Russian Pretext and the Law

Which international law did Russia violate when it annexed Crimea? Several legal scholars and observers in international affairs assessed this question in depth. The conclusion is unanimous. By relying on existing international principles, Russia's intervention in Crimea was an act of aggression.

---

[90] What I am saying is that there is a certain worldview in Russian politics. I am not sure the presence or the absence of one particular leader could change the Russian ideal.

Ashley Deeks notes, Russia violated several international laws, including Articles 2(4)[91] and 51[92] of the UN Charter of 1945.[93] The former article of the mentioned charter forbids a State intervention into another State's territories. The latter article sets up the condition for intervention, which must be the result of self-defense.[94] Ben Saul notes that Russia cannot claim self-defense since the Ukrainian army did not fire any shots toward the Russian State.[95]

The Russian State alluded to the Responsibility-to-Protect[96] (also known as the "R2P doctrine") when it claimed that it felt compelled to protect Russian-speaking population in Ukraine. But this argument succumbed

---

[91] Article 2(4) of the UN Charter of 1945 stipulates that states should not engage in any threats or uses of force against other states.

[92] Article 51 of the UN Charter of 1945 stipulates that only in the case of an armed attack or self-defense can a state uses force against other states.

[93] Ashley Deeks, "Russian Forces in Ukraine: A Sketch of the International Law Issues," Lawfare, accessed September 3, 2015, https://www.lawfareblog.com/russian-forces-ukraine-sketch-international-law-issues.

[94] The UN Security Council also stipulates the conditions under which a state might be authorized to use force against other states. The Council notes that only in cases pertaining to restoring peace and security can a nation use force against other states.

[95] Ben Saul, "The Battle for Legal Legitimacy in Crimea," Text, ABC News, March 3, 2014, http://www.abc.net.au/news/2014-03-03/saul-the-battle-for-legal-legitimacy-in-crimea/5294828.

[96] The R2P doctrine is an exception to the general prohibition set by the UN Charter of 1945 when it comes to use of force or unilateral intervention.

under legal (or even rationale) scrutiny. Marc Weller argues that Russia clearly violated IL when Russian military personnel entered Ukraine (the Crimea region).[97]

The doctrine known as "Rescue of Nationals Abroad" does not necessarily justify occupying parts of a neighboring State. The doctrine of "humanitarian intervention" does not apply in this case either, for there was no humanitarian crisis in Crimea. No matter how one looks at what took place in Ukraine, there is no possible excuse, which the Russian State could evoke to explain its actions. Yet, IL institutions could not punish Russia, at least not severely, for its actions in Crimea.

Other observers espoused an unorthodox perspective in the debate. Many viewed the Russian intervention in Crimea under a slightly different lens. Boris Mamlyuk argues that Russia may have had legitimate concerns for the Russian-speaking population in Crimea. [98] Unlike Georgia in 2008, Russia has more evidence to support the claim that the Russian-speaking population was in danger.

The author notes that the threat of ethnic persecution or even the threat of genocide was real. Therefore, we should not undermine such possibilities. [99] Since they expelled President Yannukovich, the Ukrainian State

---

[97] Weller, "Analysis."

[98] Boris N. Mamlyuk, "Mapping Developments in Ukraine from the Perspective of International Law," *CJICL* (blog), accessed September 4, 2015, http://cjicl.org.uk/2014/03/12/mapping-developments-ukraine-perspective-international-law/.

[99] Ibid.

seemed incapable of protecting ethnic Russians from the threat posed by ultra-nationalist armed mobs.[100]

The belief in various pro-Russian circles is that Russia may have had a legitimate ground to appeal to the "R2P doctrine" to justify its intervention in the Crimean region. Nonetheless, this side of the debate was not a part of the rationale many powerful countries espoused during the crisis. From where they stand, annexing the *Crimean Peninsula* is a violation of IL. Yet, the applicability of IL in the Ukrainian crisis is still unclear.

---

[100] Ibid.

CHAPTER 11

11. SANCTIONING RUSSIA

AFTER THE UKRAINE debacle, the common view often voiced by media pundits is that we should punish Russia. Despite these positions, they did nothing tangible to punish Russia. It is not clear whether Russia itself had a preoccupation for international reprisals against its actions in Crimea. In the aftermath of the Russian incursion in the region, the international community scrambled to find a unified voice.

Several countries, notably the United States and Great Britain, one-sidedly assessed economic sanctions against Russia. However, these sanctions had unintended results in the region. Russia retaliated by reducing (or threatening to reduce) its exportation of various products, including oil (petroleum) and natural gas distributions.

Because of the sanctions the international community imposed on the Russian State, some might say that many European nations suffered economically. Many countries in that part of Europe rely on Russia for their own economic survival. Their dependence on Russia in various aspects is undeniable. Perhaps that is why international sanctions against Russia have had little or no effects on the behavior of the Russian State as a whole.

Russia continues to act belligerently in Eastern Europe. The American State Department routinely echoed they have proof that Russia is fermenting various separatist movements in the region. Still, they did nothing to cut off the country's military might and political influence in Eastern Europe. But could they have done otherwise?

Another proof worth pointing out here is that Russia violated IL when its military entered Ukrainian territory. It used force to enter Ukraine. It eventually captured Crimea without any provocation. There should not be any gray area about how international institutions should have reacted. Again, this is not what took place.

The international community is yet to take a clear position (or a decisive action) against the Russian State. What does that say about the state of IL? Some might say that it aggravates IL as a powerful legal instrument.

Effects of International Law

In assessing IL, a reasonable point of departure is to discover the extent to which international rules or principles have an independent effect on the behavior of States. Arguably, IL has little or no bearing on State conducts. In its present form, IL is nearing a stage of irrelevance, expressly when it comes to stopping powerful States, just as Russia, from engaging in wanton aggressions against other States, namely Ukraine.

While the drawbacks of IL were obvious in the recent debacle between Russia and Ukraine, another prominent case is worth pointing out in the debate. In 2003, the weakness of IL was also in exergue. In this case, international institutions were powerless before President George W. Bush's determination to invade Iraq and to rid the country of its supposed stockpile of Weapons of Mass Destruction (also known as *WMD*).

Even though most UN observers were not certain on whether Iraq had *WMD*, no one could stop the United States from going to war in Iraq. Despite the fact that the presence of an imminent threat to the US was not credible, the Americans invaded Iraq anyway. Several international institutions sided with the American government, that is, until it became plain that there were no *WMD*'s in Iraq.

Few observers would refute the notion that the Iraq War was a mistake. The sad reality is that few Western leaders would admit that this war led to enumerable lost of lives and countless human rights violations. Because of the war, many civilians lost their lives senselessly.

The international community had a responsibility to protect the Iraqis against that military aggression. Yet, many international institutions were powerless to stop the Bush administration in their search to invade Iraq. This is a powerful testament of the importance (or the lack of that) of IL. What could explain that reality? I would argue that it is a lack of clear enforcement machinery.

The Enforcement Dilemma

In 2003, the UN could do little—or nothing, depending on which side of the debate one stands—to stop the Iraq war.

Many of its members became part of the casualties, which resulted from the conflict. Even in the aftermath of the war, international institutions could do nothing to protect the Iraqis against the sectarian violence that plagued the country. It was total chaos.

After the *Abu Ghraib* scandal, it became clear to most people that protecting human rights was not the priority of international bodies, namely the UN. No international institution raised a finger to exert any form of control over the treatments of prisoners of war,[101] many of whom they captured both on and off the battlefield. It was obvious that the Iraqis had no legitimate recourse against the United States.

At the United Nations, one could make the case that nobody cared about the treatments of war prisoners in other places, including in Guantanamo. No one care much about the tortuous interrogation techniques and imprisonment procedures that were in vogue back then. There was a blatant discount toward the systematic violation of human rights, which was *indispensable* during that time.

Just like Russia, the United States is a powerful State. The country is an influential member of the UN Security Council. The extent to which international principles could have deterred the United States from misbehaving in Iraq is not clear.

---

[101] The Abu Ghraib scandal was a prisoner abuse scandal that erupted between 2003 and 2004 in Iraq. United States Military personnel and CIA officers were involved in human rights violations against several Iraqi prisoners held at the Abu Ghraib prison.

This brings up several interesting questions, one of which I posed recurrently throughout this book. That is, what is the degree to which IL is important? How could it affect the State actor whose actions are immoral? Is there a difference between those who undermine international rules by minimizing them and those who flagrantly break them?

An answer to consider is that IL has little to no bearing in world politics. It would be naïve to expect that those who often violate international principles would also have esteem for IL. Those who enforce international legal principles, most often, violate such rules when it is convenient. Such actors would never disown their own practices. This is what I call the enforcement dilemma.

On the one hand, several States gathered and adopted some sets of laws, which must govern the international order. A blatant hypocrisy is worth pointing out in their approach to the laws they passed. They seldom honor their own principles.

As Ranhilio Aquino notes, wayward States justify their violation of *International Law* by evoking some principle of law. [102] The author further notes this is precisely what characterizes the laws of the international. That is, the justification for violating the law is the only currency of their misconduct. [103]

---

[102] Fr. Ranhilio Aquino, "North Korea and International Law," Manila Standard, September 1, 2017, http://manilastandard.net/opinion/columns/pens-es-by-fr-ranhilio-aquino/245889/north-korea-and-international-law.html.

[103] Ibid.

States like North Korea have constantly violated IL. However, the most blatant offender of IL includes the US itself. On several occasions, the Americans "blatantly transgressed international law," echoed Aquino. [104] The problem is when a powerful member of the group violates the same laws that it helped passed, no one could say or do anything. By that logic, it could be difficult to blame Russia (or the United States) for conducts that are, often, immoral and, for lack of a better term, unconscionable.

It could be difficult to make the case in favor of IL. At the moment, it is not clear whether one State alone could (or should) prevent another from engaging in behaviors that are in violation of international rules or principles. But let me assess IL a bit deeper to clarify that view.

Applying International Law

Invading Ukraine was one reality; annexing Crimea was another. Even so, it all took place under the watchful eyes of the international community. Most Western countries do not recognize Crimea as part of Russia. That stance, I would argue here, is perhaps inconsequential.

Crimea is a *de facto* region of the Russian State. At this point, the Crimean people are under the rules of Russian authorities. Whether the international community is willing to admit that reality is meaningless.

Russia entered Ukraine in 2014, the fact remains the same; Crimea is no longer a part of the Ukrainian State. It will perhaps remain that way so long as the Russian State

---

[104] Ibid.

holds a key position in the UN Security Council. Although it was clear that Russia's actions in Ukraine were illegal, no one could evoke IL (or any international legal principle) to sanction Russia.

It is true that everyone disapproved Russia's discount for international norms. However, few could stop the Russian State in its want to annex Crimea. Not even the Ukrainian army could stop the Russian aggression, although the Ukrainian government received the supports from powerful allies, including the United States and Great Britain. After all said and done, no one could stop Russia. No one could help Ukraine.

The question is what they could do to prevent another State from acting in the same way that Russia did. Answers are not clear. It is undeniable that they did nothing, at least in practical terms, to stop Russia from seizing Crimea. When events like that occur in the world, it undermines IL further.

The belligerent approach of the Russian State underlies the fragility of IL. One thing was clear during the Ukrainian debacle. In this instance, international principles had little or no effect on the conducts of powerful [or Rogue] State actors. States construe their behavior follow the possibility of avoiding any real results. With Ukraine, Russian leaders seemingly gauged the international community. Perhaps they found a suitable threshold of tolerance, which they exploit for their own benefits.

Before intervening in Crimea, Russian officials clearly stated their intents to take control of the region. Foreign leaders voiced their concerns. However, that did not stop Russia. The Russian State was simply unstoppable. What that means is that IL is inconsequential for powerful nations like Russia. That reality also suggests that some countries within the international order could be unstoppable.

A few other ramifications are also worthy of note. For instance, if IL could not stop powerful nations from misbehaving on the world stage, that would also signal this legal tool, at least in its existing form, could not regulate State behaviors. We could make the case that international law may not be enough to prevent a third global catastrophe, at least militarily. On the other hand, this prospect should also be alarming to any sane observer.

CHAPTER 12

12. UNDERMINING INTERNATIONAL LAW

INTERNATIONAL LAW MAKES sense in theory. Few sound-minded person would question the legitimacy (or the legal authority) of international institutions. The problem is that the useful purpose of IL, international rules, and universal principles remain a chimerical effort.

In practice, IL is a disjointed field of law. It is empty of a clear body of laws. It lacks an effective enforcement contraption.

Unlike other faces of law, IL is similar to a tool (or a legal instrument) that many people used to call attention to international-related problems. Nevertheless, as a field of law, IL does not have the capacity to solve the problems it identifies. In that sense, most States have no real duties to obey IL.

The weak nature of IL could be obvious by examining its real-world effects. We must understand that relying on the premise that international legal doctrines are unreliable in nature. Such laws have no real enforcement methods. If the enforcers are also the violators, then such enforcement could only be reckless. The effects of such enforcement could only be unpredictable. International law enforcement could be the result of the power difference between the enforcer and the State that such enforcement must come about in the end.

Enforcing International Laws

It is true that Russia violated international rules when it annexed Crimea. The greatest offense, some might argue, was Russia's illegal entry into Ukraine territory. By referring to what we discussed thus far, would it be fair to cast Russia as the only offender of international principles? The answer is…it depends.

We could argue that most powerful nations seem determined to ignore IL when it does not fall in line with their interests. There are also those that are more likely to undermine international principles when such laws hinder their interests. Even international institutions, such as the United Nations (as an organization) or the UN Security Council itself, undermine their own principles when it suits their purpose.

Who could enforce IL against the actions of the United States? Let us consider Iraq and Afghanistan further. There had been many human rights violations in these places.[105]

---

[105] See the Watson Institute International and Public Affairs (The cost of War) to learn more Watson institute for international and public affairs, "Human Rights and Civil Liberties," March 2015, http://watson.brown.edu/costsofwar/costs/social/rights.; See also Nicholas Mercer, "The Truth about British Army Abuses in Iraq Must

Yet, few people could stand and denounce such violations with the expectations that they would impugn some form of punishments to the nation or nations responsible.

We could consider the United Nations itself. This entity took part in several misconducts in many of the countries it oversaw. In 2005, Owen Bowcott notes that report reveals shame of UN peacekeepers.[106]

Let us evoke the Republic of Haiti to explain the earlier understanding. In this instance, the UN is responsible for several atrocious conducts in that impoverished nation.[107] Many of these actions are criminal in nature. Yet, there had been no reparations for the Haitians, whom experienced the actions taken or omitted by UN officials (or UN employees). Who could force the UN to compensate the Haitians victimized by their actions? Which law Haitians should (or could) evoke against the UN? I am not sure how to answer.

One of the most egregious conducts that many reproach UN personnel in Haiti is the systematic rape of young men and women in that embattled Caribbean

---

Come Out," *The Guardian*, October 3, 2016, sec. Opinion, https://www.theguardian.com/commentisfree/2016/oct/03/british-army-abuses-iraq-compensation.

[106] Owen Bowcott, "Report Reveals Shame of UN Peacekeepers," *The Guardian*, March 24, 2005, sec. World news, https://www.theguardian.com/world/2005/mar/25/unitednations.; Also see Colum Lynch, "U.N. Faces More Accusations of Sexual Misconduct," March 13, 2005.

[107] See Sofia Lotto Persio to lean more Sofia Lotto Persio, "After 13 Years and Several Scandals, U.N. Votes to End Mission in Haiti," April 13, 2017, 13, http://www.newsweek.com/minustah-mission-haiti-un-peacekeepers-scandal-583490.

country. The sexual problem is an issue that the United Nation's Security Council itself openly recognized.[108] Yet, no one could get any form of justice against this international entity. The question is why that is the case.

What is more, UN officials recognized the institution's role in introducing Cholera in Haiti. [109] The cholera outbreak led to the death of thousands of Haitians.[110] Yet, the organization refused to compensate the victims. It is plain to see that the UN is cynical, at least when it comes to IL. Does that mean that the UN, at least as a global

---

[108] See the 2006 report by the United Nations Security Council's own report to learn more. SC/8649 Security Council, "Problem of Sexual Abuse by Peacekeepers Now Openly Recognized, Broad Strategy in Place to Address It, Security Council Told. Meetings Coverage and Press Releases," February 23, 2006, http://www.un.org/press/en/2006/sc8649.doc.htm.

[109] Please see the following publications to learn more: Jonathan M. Katz, "U.N. Admits Role in Cholera Epidemic in Haiti," *The New York Times*, August 17, 2016, sec. Americas, https://www.nytimes.com/2016/08/18/world/americas/united-nations-haiti-cholera.html; Somini Sengupta, "U.N. Apologizes for Role in Haiti's 2010 Cholera Outbreak," *The New York Times*, December 1, 2016, sec. Americas, https://www.nytimes.com/2016/12/01/world/americas/united-nations-apology-haiti-cholera.html; SG/SM/18323-GA/11862 Security Council, "Secretary-General Apologizes for United Nations Role in Haiti Cholera Epidemic, Urges International Funding of New Response to Disease. Meetings Coverage and Press Releases," December 1, 2016, https://www.un.org/press/en/2016/sgsm18323.doc.htm.

[110] The current death toll has been tallied around 9,200. But that amount could exceed the official tally. To learn more, see Rick Gladstone, "Cholera Deaths in Haiti Could Far Exceed Official Count," *The New York Times*, March 18, 2016, sec. Americas, https://www.nytimes.com/2016/03/19/world/americas/cholera-deaths-in-haiti-could-far-exceed-official-count.html.

body, is superior to the law? Once again, I must admit that I am not sure how to examine this issue, at least not objectively in this case.

Could we say that UN officials made a calculated decision to undermine the rights of the Haitians victimized by their actions? Perhaps the answer is yes. Perhaps it was not the case at all. The question remains idem. What could the Haitians do to seek reparations from the UN? This is where the issue is murkiest.

I understand that some of the previous examples pale in comparison to what took place in Iraq. They do not match the atrocities that took place in other parts of the world or even in Crimea. It would be naïve not to consider the decision, which motivated the UN to avoid any liability for their misconducts in Haiti.

It would also be naïve to think that Saddam Hussein would not have used WMD if he had such an arsenal at his disposal. This is precisely the reason, I would echo, we need international standards. This is the reason there ought to be a body that controls conducts within the international system. This is why we need IL.

Nations such as Iran and North Korea nourish sinister intents when they seek nuclear weaponry. One could argue that these nations do not always have the interest of world peace in mind when they engage in their pursuit for nuclear capacities. We could not refute their argument for security concerns (both regionally and globally). Some of them are facing an existential threat from powerful nations.

Israel is a powerful nuclear nation in the Middle East. In recent years, this country has conducted itself in ways that many observers make out as reckless, at least militarily.

As much as Israel may need to protect itself against other nations in the region, others may also have a need to protect themselves against Israel. The potentiality for a larger conflict between Israel and its enemies is not a fantasy.

It is not a matter of "if" there would be a major conflict in the region. Rather, it is a matter of "when" such a conflict will happen. Nonetheless, it is not clear the extent to which such a conflict, when it happens, would not expand worldwide. It is not clear the degree to which the UN could mitigate the conflict. So far, the UN has only put resolutions against the State of Israel and *Rogue Palestinian* actors for their conducts in the region. This is the reality of IL in that part of the world.

A significant danger to world peace is worth pointing out in the debate. The Americans support Israel in every way possible. It is as if the Israelis could do no wrong. Just the same, Russia has many allies in the Middle East, including the Iranian State itself. The question worth pondering over is what would happen if a major military conflict were to erupt between Iran and Israel. It is probable that the Americans would side with Israel. The same, the Russians would probably side with the Iranians.

Another relevant question is whether the conflict could intensify to a point where it would no longer be between Israel and Iran. If that event were to happen, would it become the affair of the United States and Russia? Would there be a third party to mediate between the Americans and the Iranians? I am not sure anyone has the answer. From the looks of the reality on the ground, I doubt that the UN would be able to stand between the Americans, the Russians, and their potential enemies or allies.

Then, I am asking again; what role international law could play in promoting peace in the world? Most observers are skeptical. I am skeptical as well. In any case, there is always a need to stop Rogue Nations from engaging in conducts that could put into question the integrity of world peace.

The question worth asking is who such a nation should be. Who should be in charge of protecting the world against despotic leaders or Rogue State actors? Again, I am not sure. I would say this much; I would prefer some set of rules, which are applied equitably or not arbitrarily. I would not want to legitimize the same actions that law enforcers disown or are seeking to prevent others from undertaking.

To echo a previous inquiry, how we should expect to enforce IL when the enforcers are, more often than not, the violators of international norms, rule, and principles. Who has the moral superiority to impugn blame to other nations, including a State like Russia? Once again, I will let you be the judge of that. What is obvious is that the likelihood for a Third World Conflict is not farfetched. This would be the case particularly if we were to look at the way this tool functions.

Deterrence Power

A tangential facet of my position is that IL could have some limited effects on State behavior. Such effects might be about the State position within the international order. IL has little or no effects on powerful countries. States that enjoy little or limited international status, with military or economic powers, must uphold international rules.

Those States must not only obey international norms, but they must also experience the effects of not doing so. This reality makes IL a fickle legal instrument, at best. But it only applies when force could not prevent its application.

The States that can exert some form of authority over other States would do so without fear of reprisal. IL could also fix the behaviors of those States. For instance, a State that holds a seat at the UN Security Council might be embolden to pose an act or might omit a conduct or an action whenever it suits its needs.

Another facet of the limits of IL worth noting here is the funding issue. Most international institutions receive financing from powerful States. Such States have the means to enforce IL. They would do so whenever such laws are convenient and not damaging to their long-term goals. When a powerful State violates international norms, the effective enforcement of international rules is almost impossible. Perhaps this was the reason Russia annexed Crimea with little or no regards for IL. Perhaps this might explain the reason Russia thinks that it holds ownership of the region with little or no fear of reprisal.

Understanding the limits of IL might help clarify some of the reasons the international community stood idly by and let Russia took possession of Crimea. Perhaps there were fewer restorative actions, which powerful nations, such as the United States, France, and Great Britain, just to name a few, could do to stop Russia. Perhaps they understood their limits in the crisis. Perhaps they understood the potential risks.

Russia wanted to annex Crimea. The Russians did not hide their intents to do anything to reach their goal. In the end, there was not much the international community could have done, short from using force, to regain control of the problem.

Ukraine was on its own. As a result, many Ukrainians were defenseless before the Russian aggression. For the Ukrainian people, there was no recourse; there was no way out.

International institutions, such as the UN or NATO, could do nothing to help the Ukrainian people. International laws were grimly ineffective in that part of the world. This is the reality of the international order.

We could sum up what happened in Ukraine in one way. It was the reason of the strongest. In this case, Russia was the strongest. Even Western powers recognized this reality.

Despite their vigorous protests, they eventually backed down. Western powers recanted their threats. They bowed before Russia's military might. In doing so, they recognized Russia's regional dominance. They also acknowledged that Russia has a political influence across Eastern Europe.

What happened in Crimea had also taken place in other parts of the world, though not as flagrant. The problem is that the international community was incapable of impugning any real sanction against Russia. From here, Russia's aggression could go unpunished forever.

This possibility, I would also contend, would set the wrong precedent in world affairs. The implication worth pointing out here is that it would bolster Russia's stance in world politics. This likelihood would irrefutably underline the failure of international institutions. It would highlight how IL is relevant, at least as an effective legal instrument to regulate State conducts.

Looking Ahead

The pervading belief is that international institutions must condemn belligerent States, markedly when they engage in bad conducts. I agree. Many people share the belief that international bodies, such as the UN, must not excuse behaviors that might encourage human rights violations. I also agree.

What is it that we could do, at least in practice, to deter *Rogue States* from misbehaving? This is where the debate is problematic. There is not a universal approach.

I would say this much though. It is not enough for the UN to release resolutions, which condemn actions that violate IL. There ought to be a means of enforcement, which could deter bad behaviors. However, such an instrument would have to apply universally.

It does not make any sense to have laws that condemn certain conducts when certain States engage in them. IL often becomes inconsequential when powerful nations engage in the same conducts this legal tool must prevent or punish. This practice weakens IL at its core. It makes it harder to force belligerent nations, not necessarily powerful nations alone, to uphold the rule of law when the enforcers of such rules have little or no regard for them.

As long as we live within an international order, which is the result of rules and controls, there is always going to be a need for IL. Such laws, I would further insist, must have similar enforcement effects whenever it certain that somebody violated them. There should be no exceptions.

Having an international legal instrument is important. This is perhaps the only way for powerful nations to enjoy any sense of moral superiority in the world. This is also the best way to improve IL, at least as a deterrent apparatus against *Rogue States* or leaders whose temperament, which we could describe as "Mad as a March hare." Such a legal principle must be fair. Its application must be equitable both in theory and in practice.

CHAPTER 13

13. THE NEED OF INTERNATIONAL LAW

I POINTED OUT a series of issues about international legal principles in this text. These issues could explain the reason applying IL can be a daunting task. They could also explain the nature of the problems that pervade the global legal system itself. But the reality is more complex than that.

I also made a few arguments refuting the usefulness of IL. Nevertheless, important questions remain. That is, aside from the notion that there is no rule of law within the international community, why many consider Russia a threat to global peace? The same, what might explain the reason the Russian State appears so antagonistic toward its neighbors?

At this point, I must admit that there are no clear answers. Thus, finding an explanation, which might explain Russia's conducts in Eastern Europe or in the world for that matter, is nearly impossible. Perhaps we might have to investigate the country's history in Eastern Europe. But this was not our aim here.

In this book, I did not delve in certain facets of the debate. Although the work featured a number of historical accounts about Russia, it did not disentangle the policy ramifications of such a history. This work centered mainly on the nature of Russia's conducts in Europe. The goal was to explore the effects of such conducts for world peace.

Russia's recent actions in Eastern Europe suggest that Russian leaders nourish malign intents for the region. When it comes to the security and the peace of the Baltic States, notably in Ukraine, many observers regard Russia's mischievous behaviors as a direct effort to undermine international norms. I would share a similar view. We could understand Russia's goal as a way to boost regional control and global dominance.

Is it fair to blame Russia as the sole culprit for the downfall of the Ukrainian State? Is it fair to blame Russia for the failure of IL? I would say no.

Indisputably, Russia played a role in creating a chaotic atmosphere in Eastern Europe. There is fear in the region. Russia undermined IL in every aspect. Other actors have also played a significant role in the Ukraine debacle.

The Need for Enforcement

The absence of a plan for setting up international rules and global agreements poses a serious problem for States to honor the agreements or treaties they signed. As discussed in chapter 8, Russian leaders withdrew from the treaty they signed with Ukraine. This act, in and of itself, perhaps from the Russian vantage point, gave them the legal stance or the moral ground they needed to invade Ukraine.

This reality highlights that signing the treaty had no real meaning for Russian officials. Since nations are free to abdicate or to renounce agreements, enforcing IL, norms, or rules depends on the extent to which a State wants to uphold such rules. Therefore, we could not examine IL only by referring to a mere signed treaty.

Although many observers consider treaties a form of a contract,[111] their effects and even their enforcements, I would argue, do not always mirror that of a contract under the purview of common legal maxims. A treaty does not necessarily have the same weight as a contractual agreement. What might explain that incongruity? As echoed throughout this text, it is the lack of a clear enforcement technique for IL.

The Russian State never hid its intents to invade Crimea. The international community seemed perplexed

---

[111] To learn more about treaties as contracts, please see the following pieces of literature. Duhaime's Law Dictionary, "Treaty Definition," accessed November 24, 2018,
http://www.duhaime.org/LegalDictionary/T/Treaty.aspx; Curtis J. Mahoney, "Treaties as Contracts: Textualism, Contract Theory, and the Interpretation of Treaties," *The Yale Law Journal* 116, no. 4 (January 2007): 676–881; Marci Hoffman and Caitlin Hunter, "Treaties and International Agreements," International & Foreign Law Librarian, UC Berkeley Law Library, June 19, 2013,
https://www.law.berkeley.edu/library/dynamic/guide.php?id=65; Srikanth Hariharan, "Distinction between Treaty and Contract The Principle of Proportionality in State Contractual Actions in Investment Arbitration," *The Journal of World Investment & Trade* 14, no. 6 (January 1, 2013): 1019–54, https://doi.org/10.1163/22129000-01406006.

about a time to intervene. To this day, Russia's violations in Ukraine remained unsanctioned in the true sense of the term *"Sanction."* We could not make the argument that Russia is not the exception to an unstated understanding within the international order. That is, those who make these laws are not necessarily subject to them. Sadly, this is the trademark of IL.

Perhaps certain members of the international community felt powerless before the extent of the Russian aggression in Ukraine. Perhaps, there was a sense of caution not to provoke a global conflict. In any event, Ukraine was the only victim.

The Ukrainian people had little or no legal recourse against Russia. The international community sat this one out. It implicitly or directly, depending on which side of the debate one stands, accepted the Russian behavior and rewarded Russia by not doing anything tangible to stop it. This is a sad reality for defenseless countries.

Annexing Crimea could have an irreversible effect on global peace. It has the potential to embolden Iran or North Korea to seek nuclear powers at all costs. Who could blame them? The Russian incursion in Ukraine highlighted the flaws of IL. It did so in many aspects.

Russia annexed Crimea under the nose of the UN and NATO. That shows the weakness of the international community. It proves that some countries could be rewarded for engaging in aggressive conducts. This is so particularly if the aggressor were to enjoy the right position within the UN Security Council. Further, it shows that we could not use IL to deter *Rogue States* from misbehaving. It also underlines the need for a nation to be able to defend the self against a powerful nation.

The nature of IL (or the characteristic of the international legal order) is the sole responsible for the reality of many nations with the types of actions taken or omitted. It dictates the kinds of behaviors, which powerful nations or those seeking to shield themselves from the actions or the omissions of powerful, but also belligerent, nations would be willing to tolerate. Thus, IL often plays a role in the chaotic nature of the international order itself.

Let me reiterate that I am not arguing against the rule of law internationally. There is a need for IL. I do not think the world would be a better place without rules. In truth, I must admit that the notion of IL comes from sound principles. Nonetheless, my concerns lie in the way we apply such rules or principles.

Domestic Law versus International Law

According to the anarchic worldview, the world is chaos. By that logic, there is not a clear authoritative arrangement within the international order. This reality brings up an interesting question. That is, why do we have international rules in effect? Why do we have IL in the first place?

What sets domestic laws apart from IL is their degree of enforcement. The fundamental underpinning of every domestic law is that such a law must regulate relations among the subjects of a clearly defined territory. Why is it that IL does not fall under the same category?

There should not be any difference between domestic laws and IL. It is true that domestic laws are restrictive in nature. Of course, we could not say the same about the extent of international legal maxims or the enforcement tool of IL.

An important nuance is worth pointing out in the debate. Although there are territorial demarcations in the world, there exists no clear sovereign nation in charge of world order. Thus, it could be said that no one nation owes loyalty (or no nation owes any sense of obedience) to another nation or a global entity. In making that argument, I understand that such a reality does not deny the need for IL, at least for the sake of global peace.

IL is part of the anatomy of the global order itself. We could trace the foundation of IL all the way back to past customs and traditions, which endured, for lack of a better term, the test of time. But times are different now. The interests of nations are more ferocious than they were, say, after the Second World War.

There could not be an international entity, which could enjoy some form of power similar to the United Nations. Presently, there is no consensus within the international order. The problem is that the world's borders are more open than they were, say, six decades ago.

Today, the world is more consistent with geography and economy. Still, the world is also less likely to speak in a unique voice as the way it used to be, notably when it comes to countries seeking to preserve national interests. For that reason, the reach of IL must consider the reality of the world today.

Positive International Law

International law is positive law in its most obvious sense. I argued in a previous text (see *Natural Law: Morality and*

Obedience) that there is little or no difference between natural law (as now understood) and positive law (as now defined). Granted, I am not sure where to lump IL, at least as a legal instrument. The reality is that this tool seems insignificant in many aspects. Regardless, such an approach to legality is an offshoot of positive legal maxims.

To reiterate a previous viewpoint, there is little or no consensus about the limits of IL. While there is an agreement about what such a legal maxim is (or should entail), there is no clear enforcement agent. Obedience to IL is not always an expectation. By relying on that understanding, I am not sure of the degree to which we could refer to IL as an effective legal tool, which come from sound legal doctrines.

I would take this argument a bit further though. I would say that this form of law only applies in context and not necessarily in substance. It is not surprising that IL is seldom enforceable.

There is no incentive for obedience within the international order. It may come down to the need for survival itself. If obeying the law would contribute to a nation's survival, I am sure that such a nation would uphold international principles no questions asked. On the other hand, if the nation is already powerful and make out another as a threat, obeying international rules would seem counterproductive. Therefore, obedience to IL is always a calculated choice; it is nothing else.

Other times, it might be the result of the reason of the strongest. It is not surprising that nations compete for global dominance. That pursuit is not by coincidence. I would argue that obedience could be a form of assurance for long-term survival within the global order itself. No law could change that reality.

Assuming that nations would always agree to live in peace and harmony, some might also feel that they have an obligation, a moral obligation that is, to obey the principles that they agreed to uphold. Nonetheless, these nations could only hold a higher moral ground within the global community by honoring their agreements. Otherwise, a nation, no matter how powerful it might be within the international structure, would open itself to scrutiny, just as I sought to do it in this book.

As announced on the outset of the manuscript, this book was not exclusively about the Russian State itself. I mentioned several other nations, whom, in my view, are not that different from Russia in how they conduct themselves within the international order. Still, there is a need for the law. There is a need for rules within the international structure. There is a need for IL.

The reality of the international order makes it impossible for the law to grow organically. Echoing this view does not deny the fact that the law is typical for long-term peace. The law is fundamental for order.

Undermining the law, while laboring for peace, is absurd. True, international legal principles come from men; IL also comes from positive legal maxims. Nonetheless, international legal principles must invite a genuine need for obedience.

In saying all that, I understand the reality of International Law. I understand why certain heads of states felt cautious to allow their country to find itself at the mercy of international institutions or institutions, such as the UN. We must rethink the foundational principles of that institution.

In its present format, international laws could annul domestic laws. No sound minded Political leader would stand for that. Perhaps this is precisely the reason International Law, at least as a legal instrument, is so controversial and, at times, inconsequential.

Final Words

CLOSING SEGMENT

CONCLUSION

EVEN THOUGH I mentioned the actions of several other countries, the argument I sought to echo in this book is that Russia enjoys too much influence both in Eastern Europe and within the international community itself. To reiterate, this book was not about the Russian State itself. I used Russia as an example to illustrate the precocity of international legal principles.

Presently, few people would deny that Russia plays an important role in international politics. However, its domestic policies often affect its neighbors in a negative way. The country inherited the USSR's power and influence within the international order, distinctly within the United Nations Security Council. Sometimes, that can be a problem for both regional stability and global peace.

Most observers fear that any behaviors Russia indulges itself regionally could have serious effects globally. This fear is in part because Russia is an important player in world politics. Russia is among the institutions that regulate the conduct of nations. Yet, Russia itself often behaves badly on the world stage.

Russia is not alone in its search for regional (if not global) dominance. We must note that the Russian State is not the only powerful nation that seems determined to follow its own interests. Russia is not the only country, which regularly engages in mischievous behaviors. Thus, it would not be fair to single out Russia.

No one country could claim any sense of moral superiority in the world. Most nations misbehave either on the world stage or domestically. The major problem is that there is not a clear legal instrument, which could deter *Rogue States* from misbehaving. We often use the law of the international as a trampoline for misconducts.

Many observers have wondered about the extent to which international institutions could control the Russian State. While answers are not clear, there is more at stake. Russia is part of a corollary of problems, both regionally and globally, which could spill over in other parts of the world; they may lead to a larger conflict.

There is also a sense that Russia is increasingly becoming untamable. The country has often oversteps its regional authority. In doing so, it often ignores international norms. In various places in the world, notably within the Eastern European corridors, there are concerns about Russia's surging power and influence. Such concerns, I would argue, are unquestionably necessary.

Understandable State of Panic

There is an understandable fear toward the Russian State. Nations that used to be a part of the Soviet Union fear that Russian leaders could design any claim to undermine their sovereignty. Few people could dismiss such claims; few could argue that such concerns are baseless.

Since the beginning of the 21st century, the Russian State engaged in conducts, which we could make out as flagrant violations of basic human rights. Russia had been in conflicts with most of its closest neighbors. The State invaded a few nations, including Georgia. Crimea is its latest takeover. Where or when does it stop? I am not sure.

Thus far, the Russian Government has not suffered the effects of its actions. The Russian State, some might say, seems undeterred and unaffected by international norms. Sanctions alone do not have an immediate effect on Russia. The question is why that is the case. My answer is that IL is too weak.

International institutions are inconsequential in world politics. Often, they are irrelevant. Therefore, IL, by itself, could not induce the Russian State to change its behavior. By that logic, we could argue that Russia is untamable within the global order. It would always be unstoppable, at least via this means only (that is, via international law).

Presently, is there an international overseer in the world? If not, is there a need for one? I would say no, at least so long as there is IL. We could describe the state of IL as both useful and irrelevant, depending on who seeks its enforcement. I reckon that some observers might have a different view.

In this work, I sought to answer a few questions about the nature of the international order. I sought to disentangle the degree to which a lack of adhesion to IL by some of the most powerful nations makes its applicability almost impossible. My approach here is speculative, even though I referenced several works.

We must assess IL in more detail. There is a need for a clearer picture about why, when, and how international legal doctrines should apply. The risks of a global conflict are enormous. It would not be beneficial for the planet to allow powerful States to enforce international rules as they see fit. The stakes are too high. The risks are too serious.

A New Legal Order

To be clear in my position, I am not promoting a one-world government. It was not my goal to suggest such an impression. I do not think that a new world order is even feasible in this day in age. Without doubt, some people believe this is the way of the future. I would not refute that understanding per se.

I would point out that, even those who believe in such a demarche do not always want to admit it openly. This is to suggest they are aware of the complex nature of such a demarche. A unified government is only possible via deception or deceit. I am not sure that the world would stand for such a global trickery.

There is a pressing need to have laws that create a sense of equilibrium within the international order. The world today is one mistake away from complete inhalation. There is giddiness among some nations that have the means to destroy the world, at least as we know it, to effort to protect it.

When nations misbehave, they evoke the need to uphold human rights, democracy, and the rule of law as justifications for their actions. Yet, their conducts often violate the same norms that they seek to honor. In its present design, IL is ill equipped to prevent the world from falling into complete anarchy.

Considering their organization and influence, international institutions, such as the UN, could not carry out the task of upholding world peace without provoking a global conflict, if not a *Third World War*. It is not surprising that nations, such as North Korea and Iran, are competing for military advantage within the international order. We could understand their search for nuclear power as an effort to mitigate their reasonable state of panic and their impotence within the international order itself.

I am not suggesting that I excuse the pursuit of nuclear weaponry. What I am saying is that if a nation could make it difficult for the world, that nation would do so, at least, at some point. Thus, it is the responsibility of powerful nations to lead by example. The reality is that such nations often conduct themselves in unacceptable manners within the international order itself.

Most people would contend that the only way to stop a bully is by bullying the bully himself. But this is a vicious cycle, I would argue. When a bullying victim becomes a bully, his or her conducts could become unfathomable.

It is never a good practice to incite a bullying victim to become a bully. The new bully might be fiercer than the other bully could ever be. He might become unstoppable.

The best way to stop a bully is by pointing out what is wrong in their behavior. Nonetheless, it is important to stop similar behaviors by relying on already settled rules. Thus, there is a need for a sustainable, but also equitable, legal order in the world today.

If we want a world where the rule of law prevails, we must also apply existing laws to everyone. Such laws must not only apply to those who created them, but they must also apply to those who enforce them. Further, they must apply to those who experience the effects of said laws. When it comes to IL, this is not the case at all. For instance, Russia's recent conducts in Ukraine highlight that reality.

No doubt, IL is heading in the wrong direction. Most belligerent leaders play a role in what the UN does. There is a double standard in the way this institution applies and enforces the law.

The fundamental question we should be asking is the following: Who should oversee the overseers of the world? At this point, I have no clue. But I hope that you do. If not, I hope that you will be able to come up with a convincing answer in a near future.

AUTHOR'S NOTE

THE RUSSIAN STATE has been in the news for its actions in Crimea. In this work, I revisited facets of the Russian incursion in Ukraine. While this book does not center on the crisis in Crimea itself, it examines, although not comprehensively, the reach of Russian influence in Europe.

In 2014, Russia annexed Crimea. It did so under the watchful eyes of the international community. This act, though daring, proved the limits of international institutions. Russia's actions further revealed that the rules that are supposed to guide order within the international system have little or no bearing. It was important to explore the reach of international institutions to deter a powerful state like Russia. While this book is not about Russia in itself, a good portion of the manuscript debated the most publicized actions this nation undertook recently.

You may wonder why it was important to write a book linking the Russian State and international law. Let me say right from the start that I am no expert about Russian affairs. However, I have enough academic expertise in the domain to incite a sound debate. Over the last few years, I conducted several inquiries about corruption in Russia. As a result, I learned a great deal about Russian society. Another issue is worth outlining here as well. That is, the rule of law.

The presumption is that the world must have in place sets of rules, which every nation must obey. In reality, international rule of law can be dismally ineffective. Some might even say that it is a gimmick. Certainly, international legal principles have limits. They can have little or no effects on certain countries.

The world is more chaotic than most would admit. It is more volatile than most realize. The types of transnational skirmishes that led to both the First and the Second World War are still brewing in various parts of the globe. Yet, some nations are acting as if they could contain a third global conflict by pressing on a button. Some countries have more concerns about abstract notions about the world than the reality nations face.

Meanwhile, the grievances of beleaguered nations are mounting. Still, no one seems concerns. Few want to afford much credence to suffering nations. This is a huge mistake, I would say.

It is a matter of time before survival instincts takes precedents over the need for global rationality. It is a matter of time before national interests take precedents on global needs. When that happens, this could shatter any hope for world peace. There would be no way to force a nation to remain civil.

If that were to be the case, the human species would lose it all. The devastation, the pain, and the sorrow that reality might breed would be incommensurable. That is why international law is important, however feeble it might be right now. The world needs order, at least to some extent. This is a necessary path for global peace.

While there is no better time for international rules to be as potent as they could be, they are as weak as they could get. Within the international order, the law is the only buffer that could prevent belligerent states from misbehaving. Because of the fragility of international legal principles, many states (mostly smaller nations) have no alternatives but to fend for themselves. This reality could lead to anarchy within the global order. Powerful states could continue doing as they please. This could be detrimental for the human species.

Indeed, the Russian State is on the rise. The country's power and influence have grown at a rapid pace. Russia's ascendance (both economically and militarily) has had a chilling effect in world politics. The growing fear many feel for Russia is far from being unreasonable. While that fear is mostly plain in Eastern Europe, many feel the Russian chill across the globe.

This work is not a way to voice frustrations against Russian leaders. It is not an effort to disown Russia or the Russian people. I found the crisis between Russia and Ukraine intriguing. I wanted to explore the issues further.

Keep in mind that this book is not a defense of Russia. I did not overlook the country's actions to support a particular argument. I did not seek to depict Russia under a negative light. One could argue that most Russian leaders enjoy a *"Bad Boy"* reputation in world affairs. The goal was to explore that reputation thoroughly.

Let me also point out that this compilation is part of a larger body of work, which I compiled many years ago. Considering Russia's assertion in world politics, I wanted to revisit previous finds about the subject. Keep in mind that the present installment is different from my other works in the field.[112]

The book does not examine Russia solely. It relates the actions taken by Israel, Iran, North Korea, Venezuela, and the United States. It highlighted the role these countries played in creating a negative outlook for international rule of law. The aim was to assess the degree to which international legal instruments are potent enough to prevent a third world conflict.

I argued that, in its existing morphology, IL could not preserve world peace. Considering the complex nature of the conversation, it is important to exert a bit of caution in the debate. Still, I must point out that there is an enforcement problem with IL. Applying international rules in a consistent and fair manner is almost impossible.

The main claim I echoed throughout this work is that international institutions are weak. In parts of the world, it is complete anarchy. There is no rule of law. It is the reason of the strongest. International legal principles can be difficult to enforce.

Ben Wood Johnson, Ph.D.
April 2020

---

[112] Most of my other works about Russia examine the nature of corruption in Russian society.

BIBLIOGRAPHY

BELOW IS A COLLECTION of works referenced in the manuscript. They include authors' name(s); publication title (and sub-title); publisher name(s); other links; web pages; and other references quoted either directly or by inference. This collection also includes works mentioned, but not specifically cited, throughout the manuscript.

Aquino, Fr. Ranhilio. "North Korea and International Law." Manila Standard, September 1, 2017. http://manilastandard.net/opinion/columns/pens-es-by-fr-ranhilio-aquino/245889/north-korea-and-international-law.html.

Assessing Russian Activities and Intentions in Recent US Elections. Intelligence Community Assessment. Office of the Director of National Intelligence, National Intelligence Council, 2017.

Austin, John. *Austin: The Province of Jurisprudence Determined.* Edited by Wilfrid E. Rumble. 1st edition. Cambridge ; New York, NY: Cambridge University Press, 1995.

Bater, James H., and Romuald J. Misiunas. "Baltic States." Encyclopædia Britannica, inc., January 8, 2016. https://www.britannica.com/place/Baltic-states.

BBC News, What in the world? Pieces of global opinion. "Hillary Clinton's Putin-Hitler Analogy," March 6, 2014, sec. Echo Chambers. https://www.bbc.com/news/blogs-echochambers-26476643.

Bowcott, Owen. "Report Reveals Shame of UN Peacekeepers." *The Guardian*, March 24, 2005, sec. World news. https://www.theguardian.com/world/2005/mar/25/united nations.

Buckley, Cynthia, Ralph Clem, Jarod Fox, and Erik Herron. "The War in Ukraine Is More Devastating than You Know." Washington Post, April 9, 2018. https://www.washingtonpost.com/news/monkey-cage/wp/2018/04/09/the-war-in-ukraine-is-more-devastating-than-you-know/.

Carey, John. "The United Nations' Double Standard on Human Rights Complaints." *American Journal of International Law* 60, no. 4 (October 1966): 792–803. https://doi.org/10.1017/S0002930000105883.

Carpenter, Ted Galen. "Why Russia Fears NATO." Text. The National Interest, October 10, 2016. http://nationalinterest.org/blog/the-skeptics/why-russia-fears-nato-17999.

Clover, Charles. *Black Wind, White Snow: The Rise of Russia's New Nationalism.* Yale University Press, 2016.

CNN. *Hillary Clinton On Putin-Hitler Comment*, 2016. https://www.youtube.com/watch?v=ZixsVwcofEw.

CNN Library. "Gulf War Fast Facts." CNN, August 2, 2016. http://www.cnn.com/2013/09/15/world/meast/gulf-war-fast-facts/index.html.

Collins, Eliza. "Yes, 17 Intelligence Agencies Really Did Say Russia Was behind Hacking." *USA Today (Online)*, October 21, 2016.

———. "Yes, 17 Intelligence Agencies Really Did Say Russia

Was behind Hacking." USA Today, October 21, 2016.
https://www.usatoday.com/story/news/politics/onpolitics
/2016/10/21/17-intelligence-agencies-russia-behind-
hacking/92514592/.

Curtis, Mark. "Britain's Violations of International Law." Mark
Curtis, January 23, 2017.
http://markcurtis.info/2017/01/23/britains-violations-of-
international-law/.

Daiss, Tim. "China Has Defied International Law, Now What?
Experts Speak Out." Forbes, July 16, 2016.
https://www.forbes.com/sites/timdaiss/2016/07/16/china
-has-defied-international-law-now-what-experts-speak-out/.

Deeks, Ashley. "Russian Forces in Ukraine: A Sketch of the
International Law Issues." Lawfare. Accessed September 3,
2015. https://www.lawfareblog.com/russian-forces-
ukraine-sketch-international-law-issues.

Demirel, Merve. "International Law vs. Realpolitik in the South
China Sea." *Huffington Post* (blog), March 21, 2017.
https://www.huffingtonpost.com/entry/international-law-
vs-realpolitik-in-the-south-
china_us_58d08d1ee4b07112b647313c.

Doebbler, Curtis F.J. "Why the United States' Use of Force
Against Syria Violates International Law."
www.counterpunch.org, April 7, 2017.
https://www.counterpunch.org/2017/04/07/why-the-
united-states-use-of-force-against-syria-violates-
international-law/.

Duhaime's Law Dictionary. "Treaty Definition." Accessed
November 24, 2018.
http://www.duhaime.org/LegalDictionary/T/Treaty.aspx.

Epatko, Larisa. "Once a Superpower, How Strong Is Russia
Now?" PBS NewsHour, January 13, 2017.
http://www.pbs.org/newshour/updates/how-strong-is-
russia-now/.

Gladstone, Rick. "Cholera Deaths in Haiti Could Far Exceed Official Count." *The New York Times*, March 18, 2016, sec. Americas. https://www.nytimes.com/2016/03/19/world/americas/cholera-deaths-in-haiti-could-far-exceed-official-count.html.

Goble, Paul A. "'Situation in Russia Is Rapidly Getting out of Control,' Five Leading Moscow Experts Say." *Euromaidan Press* (blog), September 16, 2017. http://euromaidanpress.com/2017/09/16/situation-in-russia-is-rapidly-getting-out-of-control-five-leading-moscow-experts-say-euromaidan-press/.

Goldman, Marshall. *Oilopoly: Putin, Power and the Rise of the New Russia*. Oneworld Publications, 2010.

Goldstein, Joshua S. *International Relations*. 6 edition. New York: Longman, 2004.

Halliday, Denis J. "The United Nations: The Embarrassment of International Law." *Medicine, Conflict, and Survival* 18, no. 4 (December 2002): 346–54. https://doi.org/10.1080/13623690208409644.

Hariharan, Srikanth. "Distinction between Treaty and Contract The Principle of Proportionality in State Contractual Actions in Investment Arbitration." *The Journal of World Investment & Trade* 14, no. 6 (January 1, 2013): 1019–54. https://doi.org/10.1163/22129000-01406006.

Herpen, Marcel H. Van. *Putin's Wars: The Rise of Russia's New Imperialism*. Rowman & Littlefield, 2015.

Hill, Fiona. "The Real Reason Putin Supports Assad." *Brookings* (blog), March 25, 2013. https://www.brookings.edu/opinions/the-real-reason-putin-supports-assad/.

Hoffman, Marci, and Caitlin Hunter. "Treaties and International Agreements." International & Foreign Law Librarian, UC Berkeley Law Library, June 19, 2013. https://www.law.berkeley.edu/library/dynamic/guide.php?i

d=65.

Hu, Elise. "After North Korea's ICBM Launch, Now What?" NPR.org, July 5, 2017. http://www.npr.org/sections/parallels/2017/07/05/53546 5234/after-north-koreas-icbm-launch-now-what.

Human Rights Watch. "Egypt: Year of Abuses Under Al-Sisi." Human Rights Watch, June 8, 2015. https://www.hrw.org/news/2015/06/08/egypt-year-abuses-under-al-sisi.

IHH Humanitarian Relief. "Falk: Double standards in international law." IHH Humanitarian Relief Foundation, February 11, 2012. https://www.ihh.org.tr/en/news/falk-double-standards-in-international-law-1472.

Intelligence, United States Office of the Director of National, and National Intelligence National Intelligence Council. *Assessing Russian Activities and Intentions in Recent Us Elections.* CreateSpace Independent Publishing Platform, 2017.

International Court of Justice. "Cases: International Court of Justice." Accessed November 24, 2018. https://www.icj-cij.org/en/cases.

Iran Business Risk. "The Islamic Republic of Iran's Violation of Treaties and Multilateral Agreements." UANI. Accessed November 27, 2018. /violation-of-treaties.

Ireland Palestine Solidarity Campaign. "Israel's Violations of International Law: A Brief Introduction." Ireland Palestine Solidarity Campaign. Accessed July 9, 2017. http://www.ipsc.ie/israels-violations-of-international-law-a-brief-introduction.

Jordan, Amos A., William J. Taylor Jr, Michael J. Meese, and Suzanne C. Nielsen. *American National Security.* JHU Press, 2009.

Kalb, Marvin. *Imperial Gamble: Putin, Ukraine, and the New Cold War.* 2nd Print edition. Washington, D.C: Brookings

Institution Press, 2015.

Katz, Jonathan M. "U.N. Admits Role in Cholera Epidemic in Haiti." *The New York Times*, August 17, 2016, sec. Americas. https://www.nytimes.com/2016/08/18/world/americas/united-nations-haiti-cholera.html.

Ledeen, Michael. "Missiles and Menaces in an Iran-Russia-North Korea Alliance." Text. TheHill, February 13, 2015. http://thehill.com/blogs/pundits-blog/defense/232717-missiles-and-menaces-in-an-iran-russia-north-korea-alliance.

Lockett, Jon. "Why Does Russia Support Syria and Bashar Al-Assad and Who Else Is Involved in the Syrian Civil War?" The Sun, October 9, 2018. https://www.thesun.co.uk/news/6006649/russia-support-syria-air-strikes-response/.

Lundestad, Eirik B., and Tor G. Jakobsen. "A Unipolar World: Systems and Wars in Three Different Military Eras." *POPULAR SOCIAL SCIENCE* (blog), February 5, 2013. http://www.popularsocialscience.com/2013/02/05/a-unipolar-world-systems-and-wars-in-three-different-military-eras/.

Lynch, Colum. "U.N. Faces More Accusations of Sexual Misconduct." March 13, 2005.

Magdy, Samy. "Egypt's El-Sissi Begins 2nd Term amid Crackdown on Dissent." AP NEWS, June 2, 2018. https://apnews.com/30269d6316484d59a6227d893d49e1f9.

Mahoney, Curtis J. "Treaties as Contracts: Textualism, Contract Theory, and the Interpretation of Treaties." *The Yale Law Journal* 116, no. 4 (January 2007): 676–881.

Mamlyuk, Boris N. "Mapping Developments in Ukraine from the Perspective of International Law." *CJICL* (blog). Accessed September 4, 2015. http://cjicl.org.uk/2014/03/12/mapping-developments-ukraine-perspective-international-law/.

Marples, David R. "Euromaidan and the Conflict in Ukraine in 2013–14." Encyclopedia Britannica, December 29, 2014. https://www.britannica.com/topic/Euromaidan-and-the-Conflict-in-Ukraine-in-2013-14-2006898.

Menon, Rajan. "How the Tumultuous '90s Paved the Way for Putin's Russia." *The New York Times*, April 10, 2017, sec. Book Review. https://www.nytimes.com/2017/04/10/books/review/who-lost-russia-cold-war-peter-conradi.html.

Mercer, Nicholas. "The Truth about British Army Abuses in Iraq Must Come Out." *The Guardian*, October 3, 2016, sec. Opinion. https://www.theguardian.com/commentisfree/2016/oct/03/british-army-abuses-iraq-compensation.

Middle East Monitor. "Amnesty: France Violates International Law by Selling Arms to Egypt." *Middle East Monitor* (blog), October 17, 2018. https://www.middleeastmonitor.com/20181017-amnesty-france-violates-international-law-by-selling-arms-to-egypt/.

Motyl, Alexander. "Putin, Just Evil Enough." CNN. Accessed July 8, 2017. http://www.cnn.com/2014/07/25/opinion/motyl-putin-is-evil/index.html.

Musili, Brian Kasyoka. "What Is a Rogue State? (WorldAtlas)." WorldAtlas, August 1, 2017. https://www.worldatlas.com/articles/what-is-a-rogue-state.html.

Myers, Steven Lee. *The New Tsar: The Rise and Reign of Vladimir Putin*. Simon and Schuster, 2015.

News, V. O. A. "US Accuses Russia of Hacking Attempts on Political Groups." *Voice of America News/FIND*, October 7, 2016.

Noble, Ben, and Philippa Hetherington. "Russia Doesn't Just Violate International Law – It Follows and Shapes It Too."

The Conversation. Accessed November 24, 2018.
http://theconversation.com/russia-doesnt-just-violate-
international-law-it-follows-and-shapes-it-too-92700.

O'Connor, Tom. "North Korea Says Nuclear Weapons Only
Target U.S., Not Russia, China or South Korea as Talks
Begin," January 19, 2018.
https://www.newsweek.com/north-korea-nuclear-weapons-
only-target-us-not-russia-china-south-talks-775589.

Office of the Historian, Bureau of Public Affairs, United States
Department of State. "The First Gulf War, Short History."
Department History, Office of the Historian. Accessed July
9, 2017. https://history.state.gov/departmenthistory/short-
history/firstgulf.

Our Documents. "Our Documents - Monroe Doctrine (1823)."
Accessed November 22, 2018.
https://www.ourdocuments.gov/doc.php?flash=true&doc
=23.

Patterson, Margot. "How the U.S. Violates International Law in
Plain Sight." America Magazine, October 12, 2016.
https://www.americamagazine.org/politics-
society/2016/10/12/how-us-violates-international-law-
plain-sight.

Persio, Sofia Lotto. "After 13 Years and Several Scandals, U.N.
Votes to End Mission in Haiti," April 13, 2017.
http://www.newsweek.com/minustah-mission-haiti-un-
peacekeepers-scandal-583490.

Press, Associated. "Hillary Clinton Says Vladimir Putin's Crimea
Occupation Echoes Hitler." *The Guardian*, March 6, 2014,
sec. World news.
https://www.theguardian.com/world/2014/mar/06/hillary
-clinton-says-vladimir-putins-crimea-occupation-echoes-
hitler.

Purkiss, Jessica, and Abigail Fielding-Smith. "US Strikes Causing
Civilian Casualties More than Double in Afghanistan." The

Bureau of Investigative Journalism, October 11, 2018.
https://www.thebureauinvestigates.com/stories/2018-10-
11/us-strikes-causing-civilian-casualties-double.

Raphelson, Samantha. "'Simmering Conflict' In Eastern Ukraine
Remains At An Impasse." NPR.org, January 10, 2018.
https://www.npr.org/2018/01/10/577104670/simmering-
conflict-in-eastern-ukraine-remains-at-an-impasse.

Rucker, Philip. "Hillary Clinton's Putin-Hitler Comments Draw
Rebukes as She Wades into Ukraine Conflict." *The
Washington Post*, March 5, 2014.
http://www.washingtonpost.com/politics/hillary-clintons-
putin-hitler-comments-draw-rebukes-as-she-wades-into-
ukraine-conflict/2014/03/05/31a748d8-a486-11e3-84d4-
e59b1709222c_story.html.

Saul, Ben. "The Battle for Legal Legitimacy in Crimea." Text.
ABC News, March 3, 2014.
http://www.abc.net.au/news/2014-03-03/saul-the-battle-
for-legal-legitimacy-in-crimea/5294828.

Schearf, Daniel. "Russia Dismisses US Hacking Allegations as
'Election Campaign Instrument.'" *Voice of America
News/FIND*, October 8, 2016.

Schrad, Mark Lawrence. "Vladimir Putin Isn't a Supervillain."
Foreign Policy (blog), March 2, 2017.
https://foreignpolicy.com/2017/03/02/vladimir-putin-isnt-
a-supervillain/.

Scott, Shirley V. *International Law, US Power: The United States'
Quest for Legal Security*. 1 edition. Cambridge: Cambridge
University Press, 2012.

Security Council, SC/8649. "Problem of Sexual Abuse by
Peacekeepers Now Openly Recognized, Broad Strategy in
Place to Address It, Security Council Told. Meetings
Coverage and Press Releases," February 23, 2006.
http://www.un.org/press/en/2006/sc8649.doc.htm.

Security Council, SC/12657. "Israel's Settlements Have No

Legal Validity, Constitute Flagrant Violation of International Law, Security Council Reaffirms, Meetings Coverage and Press Releases," December 23, 2016.
https://www.un.org/press/en/2016/sc12657.doc.htm.

Security Council, SG/SM/18323-GA/11862. "Secretary-General Apologizes for United Nations Role in Haiti Cholera Epidemic, Urges International Funding of New Response to Disease. Meetings Coverage and Press Releases," December 1, 2016.
https://www.un.org/press/en/2016/sgsm18323.doc.htm.

Sengupta, Somini. "U.N. Apologizes for Role in Haiti's 2010 Cholera Outbreak." *The New York Times*, December 1, 2016, sec. Americas.
https://www.nytimes.com/2016/12/01/world/americas/united-nations-apology-haiti-cholera.html.

Shin, Annys. "Recalling the 2013 Protests in Ukraine." Washington Post. Accessed November 21, 2018.
https://www.washingtonpost.com/lifestyle/magazine/recalling-the-2013-protests-in-ukraine/2017/11/13/f9a8ba90-ae89-11e7-be94-fabb0f1e9ffb_story.html.

Spielman, Richard. "The Emerging Unipolar World." *The New York Times*, August 21, 1990, sec. Opinion.
https://www.nytimes.com/1990/08/21/opinion/the-emerging-unipolar-world.html.

Stark, Robert. "Why Israeli Settlements Are Not a Violation of International Law." The Times of Israel, January 3, 2017.
http://blogs.timesofisrael.com/why-israeli-settlements-are-not-a-violation-of-international-law/.

Starr, Barbara, Ryan Browne, and CNN. "As US, SK Drill, Tillerson Seeks Action on NK." CNN, July 4, 2017.
http://www.cnn.com/2017/07/04/politics/us-officials-meet-north-korea-missile-launch/index.html.

Stuermer, Michael. *Putin and the Rise of Russia*. Pegasus Books, 2010.

Taylor, Adam. "Analysis: The Americans Who Think Vladimir Putin Isn't so Bad." *Washington Post*, July 28, 2016, sec. WorldViews   Analysis   Analysis Interpretation of the news based on evidence, including data, as well as anticipating how events might unfold based on past events. https://www.washingtonpost.com/news/worldviews/wp/2016/07/28/the-americans-who-think-vladimir-putin-isnt-so-bad/.

Team Novelguide. "Rise of Superpowers After WWII." Novelguide. Accessed July 8, 2017. http://www.novelguide.com/reportessay/history/general-history/rise-superpowers-after-wwii.

Tharoor, Ishaan. "Don't Forget How the Soviet Union Saved the World from Hitler." The Independent, May 9, 2016. http://www.independent.co.uk/news/world/the-soviet-union-helped-save-the-world-from-hitler-a7020926.html.

The Associated Press. "Lieberman: Iran, Syria and North Korea Are New 'Axis of Evil.'" *Haaretz*, May 12, 2010. http://www.haaretz.com/israel-news/lieberman-iran-syria-and-north-korea-are-new-axis-of-evil-1.289866.

The Bureau of Investigative Journalism. "Drone Warfare." The Bureau of Investigative Journalism. Accessed November 23, 2018. https://www.thebureauinvestigates.com/projects/drone-war.

The Editors of Encyclopaedia Britannica. "Allied Powers: International Alliance." Encyclopedia Britannica. Accessed October 31, 2018. https://www.britannica.com/topic/Allied-Powers-international-alliance.

———. "Monroe Doctrine: History, Elements, & Facts." Encyclopedia Britannica, October 26, 2018. https://www.britannica.com/event/Monroe-Doctrine.

Thompson, John M. *Russia and the Soviet Union: A Historical*

Introduction from the Kievan State to the Present. Avalon
Publishing, 2012.

Thompson, Nick. "Ukraine: Everything You Need to Know
about How We Got Here." CNN, February 3, 2017.
https://edition.cnn.com/2015/02/10/europe/ukraine-war-
how-we-got-here/index.html.

Transparency International. "Transparency International -
Russia." Accessed November 21, 2018.
https://www.transparency.org/country/RUS.

United Nations Peacekeeping. "United Nations Peacekeeping."
United Nations Peacekeeping. Accessed November 27,
2018. https://peacekeeping.un.org/en/node.

United Nations Security Council. "Members of the United
Nations Security Council." Accessed November 24, 2018.
http://www.un.org/en/sc/members/.

U.S. Department of State, Diplomacy In Action. "Iran, North
Korea, and Syria Nonproliferation Act Sanctions
(INKSNA)." Accessed July 8, 2017.
https://www.state.gov/t/isn/inksna/.

Walsh, Declan, and Nour Youssef. "As Sisi Silences Critics,
Hopes Fade That Egypt's Crackdown Will Ease." *The New
York Times*, October 15, 2018, sec. World.
https://www.nytimes.com/2018/05/23/world/middleeast/
egypt-sisi-crackdown.html.

Watson institute for international and public affairs. "Human
Rights and Civil Liberties," March 2015.
http://watson.brown.edu/costsofwar/costs/social/rights.

Welle (www.dw.com), Deutsche. "Which US Cities Could
North Korea's Ballistic Missile Hit?" DW.COM, July 29,
2017. https://www.dw.com/en/which-us-cities-could-
north-koreas-ballistic-missile-hit/a-39881831.

Weller, Marc. "Analysis: Why Russia's Crimea Move Fails Legal
Test." BBC News. Accessed September 4, 2015.

http://www.bbc.com/news/world-europe-26481423.

Wikipedia. "Baltic Region." *Wikipedia*, June 3, 2018.
https://en.wikipedia.org/w/index.php?title=Baltic_region&
oldid=844232543.

———. "Polarity (International Relations)." *Wikipedia*, October
2, 2018.
https://en.wikipedia.org/w/index.php?title=Polarity_(inter
national_relations)&oldid=862212102.

Wirtschafter, Jacob. "Abdel-Fattah El-Sissi Cracks down on
Dissent in Egypt." The Washington Times, November 15,
2018.
https://www.washingtontimes.com/news/2018/nov/15/a
bdel-fattah-el-sissi-cracks-down-dissent-egypt/.

Wolff, Stefan, and Tatyana Malyarenko. "Ukraine Is Still on the
Edge, despite All Efforts to Stabilise It." The Conversation.
Accessed November 24, 2018.
http://theconversation.com/ukraine-is-still-on-the-edge-
despite-all-efforts-to-stabilise-it-92004.

INDEX

BELOW IS a list [index] of words and other popular phrases the manuscript includes.

ABOUT THE AUTHOR

BEN WOOD JOHNSON, Ph.D.

Dr. Johnson is a social observer. He is also a multidisciplinary scholar. He writes about Philosophy, Legal Theory, and Foreign Policy. He also writes about Education (School Leadership), Politics, Ethics, Race, and Crime.

Dr. Johnson is a Penn State graduate. He holds a Doctorate in Educational Administration/Leadership, a Master's degree in Political Science, a Master's degree in Public Administration, and a Bachelor's degree in Criminal Justice.

Dr. Johnson worked in law enforcement. He attended John Jay College of Criminal Justice. He is fluent in many languages, including, but not limited to, English, French, Spanish, Portuguese, and Italian.

Dr. Johnson enjoys reading, poetry, painting, and music. You may contact Dr. Johnson by using the information listed below.

Mailing/Postal Info:

330 W. Main St. Unit 214
Middletown, PA 17057

Electronic Address:

E-mail Address: benwoodpost@gmail.com

Other Info:

Find the author (Ben Wood Johnson) on the following media platforms.

Official Twitter handle: @benwoodpost

Official Facebook Page: @benwoodpost

Official blog (Ben Wood Post) at: www.benwoodpost.com

Official website: www.drbenwoodjohnson.com

Official academic website at: www.benwoodjohnson.com

You may sign up to receive regular updates about the author's academic activities

OTHER WORKS

OTHER WORKS by Ben Wood Johnson include the following:

1. Racism: What is it?

2. Sartrean Ethics: A Defense of Jean-Paul Sartre as a Moral Philosopher

3. Jean-Paul Sartre and Morality: A Legacy Under Attack

4. Sartre Lives On

5. Forced Out of Vietnam: A Policy Analysis of the Fall of Saigon

6. Natural Law: Morality and Obedience

7. Cogito Ergo Philosophus

8. Citizen Obedience: The Nature of Legal Obligation

9. Le Racisme et le Socialisme: La Discrimination Raciale dans un Milieu Capitaliste

10. International Law: The Rise of Russia as a Global Threat

11. Être Noir: Quel Malheur!

12. L'homme et le Racisme: Être Responsable de vos Actions et Omissions

13. Pennsylvania Inspired Leadership : A Roadmap for American Educators

14. Adult Education in America: A Policy Assessment of Adult Learning